Philippians~ The Joyful Life

William W. Menzies

Radiant BOOKS

Gospel Publishing House/Springfield, Mo. 65802

02-0880

Library of Congress Catalog Card Number 81-80302
International Standard Book Number 0-88243-880-8
Printed in the United States of America

A teacher's guide for individual or group study with this book
is available from the Gospel Publishing House.

Contents

Contents

1

A Model Church

READ ACTS 16:11-40; 28:30, 31; AND PHILIPPIANS 1:1, 2

What do you tell your closest friends? You are likely to reserve your highest desires, deepest sorrows, and greatest joys to be shared with those nearest and dearest to you. Paul's letter to the Philippians is like that. It is as if God permits us to look over Paul's shoulder as he pens a warm and intimate letter of appreciation to his dearest friends.

This book is about that warm and appealing letter to an ideal community of Christians. There are no enormous problems to be solved; no impending divisions or crises imminent. Rather, this Book may be subtitled "The Gospel of Joy." It is a positive message encouraging faithful Christians to continue looking steadfastly at their risen Lord. Paul takes his friends by the hand and leads them joyfully into a deeper understanding of the Lord Jesus Christ and their relationship to Him.

The City

The church Paul established at Philippi was indeed historic, for it was the first European church of which we have knowledge. Certainly it was the first church Paul established in Europe. What kind of city was this strategic center, this "beachhead" of the Christian church in pagan Europe?

5

Philippi was situated on the strategic Egnatian Way, an important highway linking the major cities of the Roman province of Macedonia. Macedonia lay just to the north of the province of Achaia, that area now known as Greece. In 356 B.C., the father of Alexander the Great, Philip of Macedon, took the ancient Thasian city of Krenides, enlarged it, and named the new city after himself!

This fortified city, 10 miles inland from the Aegean Sea and situated on a spur of the Pangaean mountain range, was indeed a gateway to Europe from the East. In 42 B.C., on the plains below the city, Antony and Octavian defeated Brutus and Cassius. After the Battle of Philippi, Antony arranged for Roman soldiers to settle in the city. The city itself was given the special status of a Roman colony and was considered a branch of Rome itself. The citizens were proud of their citizenship; an honor available to but a minority of the inhabitants of the sprawling Roman empire (Acts 16:21)!

To the Jew First

Paul, Silas, and Luke had just had a remarkable visitation from the Lord. Acts 16:10 tells us that the Lord confirmed His will for the evangelistic party by means of a vision. Just before this, Paul and his company had been headed for Ephesus, the major city in western Asia Minor. After all, it was Paul's missionary strategy to reach major metropolitan centers with the gospel, establish a church there, and from such centers see the surrounding territory evangelized. But, although the plan was sound, the *timing* was not right, for reasons best known to the Lord.

Paul attempted to leave the central Asian cities of

Iconium, Lystra, and Derbe, taking the western route to Ephesus, over the Taurus Mountains. God checked him. Then, he attempted to journey northward, to Bithynia. Checked again! Two alternatives remained. He could retrace his steps to native Cilicia, from whence the party had come, or he could take a northwestward trade route to Troas. Of course, you know the story. Paul and his associates reached the seaport city of Troas. But what then? It was here that the Lord confirmed to them His intention that they should make the bold move into Europe.

Some Christian leaders have conjectured that this act changed the course of world history. The gospel moved west—and Europe became a Christian center. What would have occurred had the gospel gone a different direction? Who would be the missionary-sending nations of the world in that event? How different Western history would have been. Those in the Western world who have been blessed in countless ways by the impact of the gospel, in which so much of culture has been permeated with Christian values, have much to thank Paul for!

Paul and his colleagues arrived in Neapolis, the seaport of Philippi, and likely walked the 10 miles to the city of Philippi (Acts 16:11, 12).

It was the custom to prohibit "cultic" religions from practicing their worship within the city. So it was that the small Jewish gathering met outside the walls on the banks of the River Gangites. The fact that women were leading the meeting seems to suggest that there weren't 10 adult males present to constitute a quorum for a proper synagogue to function.

This was Paul's pattern—to the Jew first

7

(Romans 1:16). Upon arriving in one of the great Greco-Roman cities of the Mediterranean world, Paul's mission field, he sought first to locate the Jewish synagogue. Not only were the Jews his kinsmen, but also their knowledge of the Old Testament was an ideal springboard upon which to launch the gospel. A Biblical principle here seems to be to begin with people where they are; locating a point of contact where the truth of the gospel can be introduced.

And Also to the Greeks

At the women's prayer meeting down by the river, Paul's gospel appeal touched Lydia. She was a dry goods agent of a firm located in Thyatira, a commercial center in the province of Asia (Acts 16:14). She was a "worshipper of God"; a term used to identify proselytes to Judaism. Evidently she had embraced the Jewish religion as a gentile back in her native community, where a sizable Jewish colony is known to have existed.

Lydia was the first European convert of Paul. It is of special interest that at Philippi, Luke places emphasis on the salvation of entire households. Lydia was either widowed or unmarried, for she is described as the head of her household (Acts 16:15), all of whom evidently followed her lead in surrendering to Christ. Later, in the same chapter, the jailer and his household were likewise baptized (v. 33).

Trouble!

Following the conversion of Lydia and her household, Paul and his group were invited to make her home their headquarters. Evidently this gracious gentile woman was a person of means and influence. There is clear evidence that in ancient

8

Macedonia, the role of women was quite elevated for the times and many had positions of honor; supporting the suggestion of Luke in Acts 17:4 and 12. The church at Philippi owes a debt to this noble woman.

Paul and his companions must have been delighted to see the first converts to Christ in the city. Their joy was clouded shortly, however, by opposition. How common this pattern is in the work of God. The enemy does not relinquish territory taken from him without a struggle. A demon-possessed girl followed the Christian company about, crying out loudly their identity as "servants of the most high God, which show unto us the way of salvation" (Acts 16:17). This publicity continued for a number of days. Paul was interested in the good news being broadcast throughout the city, but not by this means! Finally, Paul confronted the girl and cast out the demon that bound her (v. 18).

The girl's tormentors, who had used her to make money for them, were outraged that Paul would deprive them of her services. They accused him of teaching things not permitted by law in the city and of creating a public disturbance. An unruly mob was aroused to demonstrate against Paul and his colleagues. The magistrates had the men stripped and beaten, and then thrown into the city jail. Luke gives a vivid description of their incarceration, including the fact that the jailed men were thrown into the maximum security ward. There they were painfully secured by having their legs fastened in stocks (v. 24).

Unjustly jailed, cast into the darkness of the inner part of the prison, their backs lacerated by the brutal Roman beating, they were unable to move because of the stocks. Paul and his companion Silas were certainly in trouble! It would have been

9

natural for these men to be discouraged, and it isn't out of the question to imagine they might have been tempted to despair. Can you imagine your own feelings in the midst of such circumstances?

Victory at Midnight!

But Paul and Silas were not forsaken. In the midst of grave difficulty, they began to sing! They knew the reality of the risen Lord. The Holy Spirit made Jesus Christ very real to them—even in the darkness of the inner prison. They had a Pentecostal prayer meeting (v. 25)!

And suddenly—divine intervention! It was not accidental or mere coincidence that, at that midnight hour, an earthquake shattered the masonry of the prison, permitting the prisoners freedom. The first thought of the jailer was that if the inmates escaped, his life would be forfeited for theirs. The distraught man was about to take his own life. But Paul called out in the darkness to him and reported that none had escaped—an almost unbelievable turn of events!

It was a great opportunity for Paul to demonstrate the Christian grace of "turning the other cheek." Instead of seizing the opportunity to gain personal satisfaction, Paul used the occasion to witness to the grace of God in his life. This magnanimous and totally unexpected response from the jailed men broke the heart of the jailer. "What must I do to be saved?" That night, a hardened gentile jailer became a new creation in Christ Jesus. Furthermore, his household was also converted.

The jailer ministered to the wounds of the men, and he and his family were baptized. It was a night to remember! They celebrated the dramatic events of that night by eating and rejoicing together, praising God for His goodness (v. 34).

The final chapter of this episode occurred the next morning. The conduct of the men during the night evidently earned the respect of the local magistrates, and an order was given for their release. But Paul made it clear that it was now *his* turn. He let it be known that in the mob action of the previous day, the magistrates had been party to the beating of two Roman citizens! Such an atrocity was a serious offense. The result was Paul was able to leave the city with dignity, and the newly founded church in Philippi was given a place of respect, rather than a mark of reproach. It is interesting to observe that just before leaving for other cities along the Egnatian Way (Amphipolis, Apollonia, and finally Thessalonica), the newly released captives returned to the home of Lydia for refreshment.

We know that Luke joined Paul at Troas, just before his arrival at Philippi, because of the introduction of the first person into the Lucan narrative at that point. When the party left Philippi, the "we" passages stop, too. They do not resume again until the third journey, when Paul returns to Philippi, perhaps 3 years later. This leads to the conjecture that Luke stayed behind to pastor the fledgling congregation in Philippi; a congregation that perhaps lacked adequate local potential leadership in its earliest phases. Some have even conjectured that Luke may have married Lydia! Of this we have no knowledge.

The Church at Philippi

Luke was a gentile. Lydia was a gentile too. In fact, the names of the church members cited in the

11

letter to the Philippians (2:25; 4:2, 3) are all gentile names. Romans 15:26, 27 suggests the converts in that area were former pagans. The church, then, was largely, if not almost totally, non-Jewish in composition. One might suspect, therefore, that all manner of gentile customs and vices would crop up in the church. This was hardly a likely beginning for a model church. However, in spite of the limited influence of the Jewish Scriptures and moral tradition, this new church developed a consistent reputation as an ideal picture of the Christian example.

Paul returned once to Philippi (Acts 20:6). On the third journey, he made a brief visit; celebrating the Passover with the Christians there. Of special significance are the diligent efforts of the Philippian church to minister to Paul's needs during his travels. It was, in reality, a missionary church. Paul was their special envoy. Time and again they sent love gifts to him; whenever they could locate him (Philippians 4:15, 16). In fact, the letter to the Philippians is a thank-you note for the generosity of this congregation. They sent not only money, but also a leading elder, Epaphroditus, when they learned Paul had been put under house arrest in Rome. Here indeed was a church characterized by the spirit of Christlike love!

Paul in Rome

Paul's first visit to Philippi was during his second missionary journey, probably about A.D. 51. His next and possibly last visit was about 3 years later, on the third missionary journey. At the end of that journey, Paul was arrested in Jerusalem in the temple. He was accused of taking a gentile into the temple, which was considered an act of sacrilege.

Untrue as it was, Paul nonetheless was detained in protective custody awaiting trial. For 2 years he was kept in a military prison on the Palestinian coast at Caesarea. His appeal to Caesar led to the adventurous voyage described in Acts 27. Finally, Acts concludes with the arrival of Paul in Rome. Permitted to live in a rented house, Paul had a degree of communication with his friends, for they could come to see him. He was in the custody of the palace guards who were evidently quartered in his house. It is likely that he was chained continually to one of them.

Late in this time of confinement, which lasted 2 more years, probably about A.D. 60, Paul penned his thank-you letter to his friends in Philippi. Earlier in his Roman confinement, Paul had sent a packet of three letters to Asia Minor: Philemon, Colossians, and Ephesians. Together with the letter to the Philippians, these four are called "the Prison Epistles."

Greetings to His Friends

It is now shortly before his release from the first Roman imprisonment. Paul has been in custody for about 4 years. To his beloved friends in Philippi he pours out his heart. No bitterness or resentment do you find in this letter. It extols the grace of the Lord. Paul testifies of God's goodness to him. From the initial greeting, a strong, positive tone of joy in the Lord is the dominate theme. Notice how many times the word *joy* appears in the letter.

Paul includes Timothy in the opening greeting. Both are called "servants of Jesus Christ," by which Paul means "we are under authority of the Lord to write to you." Paul always begins his letters

13

with an announcement of the authority by which he writes.

The *destination* is described vividly: ". . . saints in Christ Jesus which are at Philippi." The entire congregation is included, although the church leadership, the elders (bishops) and deacons, are specifically mentioned. It was a well-ordered church, with a structure outlined in 1 Timothy 3.

Verse 2 is a standard greeting, common in Paul's epistles. "Grace and peace"—greetings for all—gentile and Jew! It is significant that the *source* ofspiritual well-being, grace, and peace, is credited to God the Father and the Lord Jesus Christ. The language indicates the high estimate Paul has of the Lord Jesus. He is coequal with the Father. Paul now leads his "model church" into adoration of the risen Lord. Here is joy, indeed!

2

Improving Your Prayer Life

READ PHILIPPIANS 1:3-11

Philippians is intensely personal. More than 100 times Paul employs the first-person pronoun. By this means, he is laying bare his soul to his Philippian friends. No, it is not boasting or self-centeredness; it is testimony. He is taking his friends into his heart and sharing with them what Christ means to him.

In this passage, Philippians 1:3-11, Paul invites his readers to enter his prayer closet. He explains to them how he prays. Here is a model for prayer for Christians of all ages. Let us go with the Philippians into Paul's communion with the Lord. How does he pray? What can we learn from this intimate glimpse into the apostle's heart?

Thanksgiving

Paul was accustomed to praying. It was as natural to him as breathing. Later, in chapter 4, Paul returns to the theme of prayer. There he emphasizes *petition*, asking God for specific things (4:6). Here, the communication of the Christian with his Lord is put in the context of *thanksgiving*. Without doubt, Paul has in mind the generosity of the Philippians. He is grateful for the gift of money brought to Rome by Epaphroditus. Although he certainly appreciates their goodness to him, he makes it clear that it is really God who has used them to be a means of blessing. In his times of communion with the Lord, every time he remembers his Philippian friends he thanks God!

Supplication

Three important things are stated in verse 4. First, he is *continually* praying for them. The construction of the passage emphasizes Paul's persistent, regular intercession on their behalf. His praying was not a casual mouthing of platitudes. For him, it was serious business. It was important.

Second, Paul prays for *all* the saints. He thought of the Philippian church as a family. They were more than a group of isolated individuals. They were a family of God's people who shared a common set of values. Collectively, they engaged in spiritual ministry. It was a Spirit-led body. Each member was precious and special, but Paul well understood the great Church principle of "diversity within unity" (see Ephesians 4; Romans 12; and 1 Corinthians 12 to 14). Therefore, he prayed for the entire group as a body, as well as the individual members of the body.

Third, Paul's remembrance of them, and his prayer for them is with *joy*. How wonderful that in the midst of his suffering, the very thought of his friends flooded his heart with joy! Paul could not say the same about any other church in the New Testament world to the degree expressed here. Indeed, this was a special group of God's children for Paul. It took no great effort for him to beseech God to supply blessings for these friends.

Affirmation

It is a pattern in Paul's writings to begin his correspondence with a listing of things for which he can praise his readers. Only in the severe letter to the Galatians does Paul omit this gracious and gentle introduction. And, in verse 5, he clearly acknowledges the reason for his fond memory of his friends in Philippi. Their "fellowship in the gospel" is a sweeping statement. It is like saying to them, "Thanks for identifying fully with my passion for carrying the gospel to the world." They saw eye to eye with Paul and were supporting him at every turn. So, Paul gratefully acknowledges the contribution they had made to him. He affirms his friends.

How frequently we take for granted those who labor with us. Sometimes we do not affirm those nearest to us, even members of our families, as we ought. This is not flattery, mind you. This is sincere gratitude for actual deeds and attitudes. It is the *affirmation* that is a Christian virtue! It is a valuable component of strong, healthy, Christian relationships.

Confidence

Verse 5 contains appreciation for fellowship in the gospel *from the first day until now*. Paul acknowledges their persistent and dependable character. In the next verse, he builds on *their* faithfulness, to point out his confidence in God's faithfulness to them. Just as they had proven themselves to be dependable, so God could be depended on to "bring to completion" what He had begun in them.

Paul's prayer for them was not one of anxiety,

fearing that they would not make it. No, not at all. Because Paul knew the faithfulness of God and that the Philippians had begun well and had demonstrated consistent Christian commitment, he could pray in strong confidence for them.

There is a glimpse into the future in Paul's statement here (v. 6). "Until the day of Jesus Christ" refers to the return of the Lord. Paul had complete confidence that what God had begun in the lives of the Philippians He would carry out faithfully right up to the end of the age.

Prayer, for Paul, was not a matter of vague wishful thinking. It was not desperately grasping at straws. Not at all! Paul's prayer life was grounded in his strong conviction of who God is and what He is like. He really knew God. It is out of that knowledge that He could worship, praise, and petition his God.

The more we know about God, the more we should be able to trust Him and commune with Him. This is why we study the Bible and take time for daily devotions, reading the Word and talking to God.

The Meaning of Friendship

Verse 7 is one of the tenderest and most intimate passages in all of Paul's writings. He acknowledges that it is *right* (fitting, proper) to *think* about them. (The word *think* actually means to bear a sympathetic interest and concern. It implies far more than merely a mental exercise, for it includes the heart.) Why? "I have you in my heart." No expression in Scripture is more tender and sensitive than this. It is the kind of language a devoted parent might use in conversation with his child. It is the language of a lover for his beloved. No moonstruck sweetheart

18

ever expressed deep feeling for another more profoundly!

And why was Paul so "in love" with the Philippians? With him, they shared in God's grace in a whole range of human experiences. One such experience is that of "bonds." Incidentally, it is the frequent reference to bonds that reinforces the belief that Paul was in prison when this Epistle was written. In what way did they participate in Paul's bonds? Surely he is referring to their compassion for him in preparing an offering and dispatching one of their own, Epaphroditus, to Rome to bring it to him. He felt keenly that in this way they were indeed sharing in the gospel.

Furthermore, they were with him in his "defense and confirmation of the gospel." These words are legal terms taken from the Roman law courts of the day. The Philippians were not afraid to be identified with Paul, even while he was on trial. Paul was conscious of their support for him in his hour of crisis. It is one thing to be a friend of one whose friendship is an obvious blessing; it is quite another to be loyal to one who is in difficulty. Compassion is tested when it is costly to be identified with a friend. The Philippians were the truest kind of friends.

The Compassion of Christ

Verse 8 expresses the intense longing of Paul for the Philippians. His separation from them had been intensified by the long years of confinement. He wanted to be reunited with his converts in Philippi. They were so dear to him that, to express the depth of his yearning, he likens his heart hunger to that of the Lord himself. The term *bowels* is translated as "tender mercies" or simply "affection" in modern versions of the Bible. The ancient Near Eastern people thought of the intestines as being the seat of the emotions. (See, for example, Jeremiah 4:19.) Of course, the love of Christ for the Church is a constant theme in Scripture (Ephesians 5:25).

It is out of that kind of tenderness and affection that Paul prays for his Philippian friends. He loves them as a father, and that fatherly love is motivated by the common bond they have in Christ.

An Apostolic Appeal

For what do you pray? What do you pray for on behalf of those you dearly love? In verses 9 to 11, we have a model of an apostolic prayer. After expressing thanksgiving, Paul now cites the list of things he covets for his spiritual children. Let us examine these petitions. Perhaps we may learn *how* to pray better (James 4:3).

The highest Christian virtue is *love*. The cluster of spiritual graces listed in Galatians 5:22, 23 are all aspects of Christian love. Of the three cardinal virtues, Paul tells us love ranks supreme (1 Corinthians 13:13). Paul can pray for nothing higher for his spiritual children than that they excel in love.

The two words that describe how love is to be developed, *knowledge* and *judgment*, throw an interesting light on the nature of love. The word *knowledge*, as it is used in Scripture, refers to a mental grasp of spiritual truth; but, more than this, it expresses a reality far greater than mere head knowledge. The full Biblical meaning of knowledge is an intimate experience of God himself, made possible through His self-disclosure in Christ, and mediated to us by faith. In other words, a *personal* experience rather than *facts about* God.

Perhaps you are acquainted with someone who knows a considerable amount *about* God, but he doesn't really know the Lord in an intimate, life-changing way. When a person comes into a vital relationship with the Lord, a lot of things are seen in a whole new light. And this kind of knowledge has a "reciprocal" effect. If one really loves God, he will grow in his *knowledge* of God. And, the more one experiences or "knows" God, the more his love will deepen, not only for God, but also for others. Can you understand why Paul put this at the top of his prayer list for the Philippians?

The second word, *judgment*, means the ability to make moral judgments, to act with "wisdom." In fact, the word *wisdom* in the Old Testament was commonly translated in the Septuagint (the Greek version of the Old Testament) by the same Greek word used for judgment. It conveys the idea of *perception* or *real understanding*. Gracefulness, tact, fitness, and propriety are all implied by this word. It expresses, if you will, "living gracefully." Saying the right thing at the right time—this is one way to picture love in action, shaped by spiritual wisdom. Every Christian community needs people who exhibit these characteristics.

Verse 10 goes on to identify two results that come from the virtues for which Paul says he is praying. One is the ability to "approve things that are excellent." This means to "put to the test." This word was used in connection with the testing of coins to determine which ones were genuine. However, in this setting, it means a finer kind of discrimination. It means to make a judgment between what is merely "good" and that which is "better." So many issues in daily life are of this order. In fact, there are probably many more decisions of this type than the sharp right-versus-wrong kind of judgment. This is a noble objective for which Paul prays—that his friends might be given the spiritual maturity to distinguish the *excellent* from the *average*.

The other expected result listed in verse 10 is *transparency*. To be "sincere and without offense" carries the underlying meaning of "letting the sunlight shine through." Paul discloses by this his concern for *how* the Christian lives out his service to the Lord, in addition to *what* he does for God. After all, we witness for the Lord by our manner of living, as well as by what we say. And how frequently criticisms arise because a Christian behaves in ways that appear to others as deceptive and shabby! To be open and aboveboard in one's dealings eliminates many unnecessary misunderstandings and heartaches. The one who operates craftily and furtively betrays his basic lack of trust in the Lord. Those who really rely on the Lord can afford to live out in the open.

Again, Paul repeats the expression, "till the day of Christ." He is praying that the qualities and virtues he desires the Philippians to have will become a persistent habit of life—right up to the end of the age. He is not praying for a single "shot in the arm." No, Paul is yearning for a pattern of life, a style of living, for his friends that will endure.

The Full Gospel

The last verse in Paul's great prayer (v. 11) wraps up his expectations for the Philippians. He prays that they may be "filled with the fruits of righteousness." In the Greek text, *fruits* is in the singular and is a way of expressing the whole cluster of graces that should mark the Christian (Galatians 5:22, 23). They are all aspects of the great central virtue, love. In this passage, Paul emphasizes the *means* by which this occurs: *through* Jesus Christ. It is by grace that we are saved (Ephesians 2:8), and grace is made available by faith in Christ. The fullness of a right relationship to God, in character and power, is available to us because of Christ!

And, finally, we come to the last phrase of Paul's great prayer. Our whole reason for being is that we should be "unto the glory and praise of God." How wonderful to have a purpose for living! Here is a message for a bewildered world.

3

Dealing With Difficulty

READ PHILIPPIANS 1:12-26

Your plans have suddenly been scrapped. Your dreams, long-cherished, have dissolved overnight. Your future seems to have taken a left turn down a detour. What do you do now? Can your Christian experience, so vital since that night you settled your decision with the Lord at the altar, sustain you in the hour of crisis and disappointment?

Paul has something very important to say about this matter. He was there—where it hurts. He writes, not only with apostolic authority, but also out of the depths of his own personal experience.

Dark Circumstances

Remember that Paul wrote this joyful letter, not in the comfort and security of freedom and family, but from within the walls of prison. Although his jail was a rented house and not a dungeon, quartered in the house were Roman troops, members of the elite Imperial Palace Guard, the "marines" of ancient Rome. After all, Paul was an important prisoner. It is possible that he was chained 24 hours a day to a guard. The custom was for prisoners to lie on the floor while the guard was changed, with the prisoner straddled by a guard to prevent escape. Note the frequency in the Prison Epistles of references to "bonds" and "imprisonment."

24

And, even if Paul were not actually physically chained, and the references to "bonds" were taken metaphorically, the situation is not really changed.

Consider Romans 15, in which Paul tells his readers how he perceives his God-given mission in life. No armchair theorist is Paul; his vision soars! He would plant the gospel in the great cities of the Mediterranean world. He would move from urban center to urban center, ever westward. From his native Cilicia, his ambition reaches to Ephesus, to Greece, to Rome, and beyond—all the way to the end of the world of his day—to Spain itself.

To confine a man like Paul, burning with God-given vision and a heart that embraces the whole world, is the most painful kind of suffering imaginable. That he was unjustly accused by his countrymen and spared a lynching by the Roman troops stationed in Jerusalem, only adds darker colors to this tragic portrait. How does Paul react to a sudden reversal of well-intentioned plans? Here in the midst of stark reality, where life is lived in its rawest hours, how does the gospel shine through?

Revival in Rome!

There are two responses Paul gives to such questions. By the time he writes, the Philippian church has learned of his imprisonment in Rome. They have dispatched a representative to take a love offering to Paul, together with their expressions of concern for him. Verse 12 sets the tone. No self-pity here! There is a strong note of triumph. "Brothers, I want you to understand something." What has happened to Paul has turned out to actually *advance* the gospel.

He goes on to explain how this startling turn of

events has transpired. Verse 13 gives the first part of the answer. The Roman troops, he tells us, are chained *to him* (paraphrasing a little). And, evidently, they are responding to Paul's gospel witness, one after another. "We are having a revival!" shouts Paul. He could not have dreamed of a strategy more successful in accomplishing his lifelong ambition. Was it his aim to get the gospel to Rome? How could he have better penetrated the palace?

Yes, it took his imprisonment to have this opportunity, but Paul sees the hand of God in the midst of the darkest of life's tragedies. It is as if God has pulled back the veil of mystery just a bit so he can understand why God arranged for his bitter confinement. What Paul is reporting out of his own experience is that there are no "accidents" for God's children. He is sovereign. He can turn apparent disasters into glorious triumphs. He is an "in-charge" God! Suffering is given meaning.

Encouragement to the Fearful

Verse 14 takes us into the second part of Paul's response. His success in winning souls in the midst of confinement had encouraged other gospel witnesses in and around Rome. Prior to this, they had become fearful, as Christians no longer came under the mantle of government protection accorded Jews. The very success of Christianity had made the new movement conspicuous. And this was dangerous.

Until about A.D. 60, the Jews were given a special status in the empire. They were a *religio licita*, an approved religion. The Romans did this to avoid a direct and disastrous confrontation with the Jews. The Jews would not worship the emperor, for that was idolatry. So, a special exemption was granted to these particular people. The Romans were smart imperialists—they did not wish to antagonize subjugated people any more than necessary. As long as Christianity was looked on as merely another sect of Judaism, like the Pharisees and Sadducees, it fell under the mantle of government protection.

Now, however, Christianity was recognized as something more than just another Jewish "denomination." It was unique. And it posed a possible threat to Rome. Or so it seemed to the unstable and unpredictable emperors of mid-first-century Rome. The shadows of Nero's terrible time were lengthening. Within 5 years of the writing of Philippians, Christians were dying in Rome for the gospel. But Paul, who had learned to look death in the face, was no intimidated so easily. His courage emboldened other witnesses. And this good news he reports to the Philippians as a second reason his imprisonment should not be looked on with such gloom.

Wounded by Friends

Physical confinement is one thing; psychological pain is another. Shattered circumstances are *external*. Yes, circumstances can mean real suffering. But, even worse than external situations that overwhelm the Christian, are hurts that come through misunderstanding or actual defamation from those we trust.

We have all, in one way or another, been victimized by misunderstanding. Something inside us cries out in protest. There is a strong impulse for self-justification. "I didn't mean it that way." But, when we discover that, out of envy or jealousy, those who ought to be helpful and sympathetic are in fact opposing our best efforts—this is a heavy, crushing, soul-tearing experience. We want to fight back. That is the natural impulse. It is precisely at this point that the most powerful kind of testimony to the gospel is possible. What can a Christian do?

Paul tells us what *his* response was to the kind of situation just described. Some of the preachers and gospel witnesses in Rome were envious of Paul's influence and success. What? Do you mean some ministers of the gospel engage in slander? Sadly, yes.

We observe that the Bible does not gloss over the sordid and painful aspects of human personality. This is an important reason to trust the Bible—it is absolutely honest. David is not protected from the pen of the historian—his misdeeds are faithfully recorded. Even Paul's anger with his colleague Barnabas is included in the chronicle (Acts 15:39). No, Paul was not perfect either. We must not be guilty of painting the Early Church larger than life. In fact, the earliest churches had a full range of the troubles we experience in today's world.

So it was that in Rome, Paul was being attacked by malicious persons merely because they were envious of him. In verse 15, Paul lets the record show that not *all* the gospel witnesses in Rome were of this order, but indeed some proclaimed Christ out "of envy and strife." Here is disclosed a spirit of rivalry. How many church splits have occurred by the descendants of these spiritually immature persons! How much pain has been inflicted by the spiritually blind! Someone has said the greatest foes of the gospel lie not *outside* the church, but *inside*.

A Soft Answer

How did Paul respond to the deep, inner pain caused by the disappointing behavior of his colleagues in Rome? The answer lies in verse 18. "What then?" or "So what?" is Paul's way of shrugging his shoulders; letting the rain of envious words and actions roll off his back. What does Paul mean? He is reporting that his confidence is in the Lord. The Lord will take care of all the inequities endured in this life—if not now, in His good time; perhaps in eternity. It is not Paul's place to justify himself and to demand instant redress for his grievances. He will rejoice if the gospel is going out at all—even through an imperfect instrument.

Here is a gracious, magnanimous, large-hearted spirit. It is an expression of faith in God and an exhibition of the love of Christ. Paul would not descend to the level of his assailants. Does this not sound like the Lord's teaching in the Sermon on the Mount?

Years ago, a Sunday school teacher of mine had a similar experience. He worked in a factory, surrounded by hard, coarse-talking men. He walked away from their dirty stories; his silent witness condemning them. Angered by his behavior, these workmen attempted to humiliate him by playing mean tricks on him. They hoped to get him to break down, to retaliate, so that his witness would be hurt. After each insult, Brother Wallace would simply smile and, hurt as he was, return evil with kindness.

One day, after a particularly offensive deed had been done to torment Brother Wallace, and upon seeing his usual composed response, the foreman walked over to him. "Mister, you have something I need. Where do you go to church?" That testimony was given by that foreman in our church. "The reason I am here today, converted, a child of God, is because of the life lived at the factory by Brother Wallace."

In the fires of painful experiences, the Lord is able to give grace to turn the other cheek. No, we are not exempt from trials. But we are promised grace sufficient in the midst of trials! (2 Corinthians 12:9).

The Greatest Enemy of All

Disappointment with circumstances tests the faith of the believer. Even more difficult is the pain of misunderstanding or malicious behavior by those within the household of faith. But, there is an enemy even more fearful than these. The uncertainty of the future, and the prospect of death itself, is indeed "the last enemy" (1 Corinthians 15:26).

Verses 19 through 26 form Paul's answer to the age-old perplexity about our unknown tomorrows, about facing death. Paul, as he writes these words, is facing a supreme test. His trial, for which he had appealed, is on the docket. He will soon be called before Caesar. The outcome is not certain. He faces possible death, lifelong imprisonment or, more happily, freedom. How does he respond to this uncertainty? As you read these brief sentences, you can sense the quiet confidence of a believer who has absolute trust in his Lord. There is no fear, no hysteria, no wringing of the hands. Paul has settled the great issues surrounding life and death. He is in the hands of the Lord!

Paul begins this statement on his future by expressing appreciation to the Philippians for their prayers for him (v. 19). How characteristic of Paul. He recognizes that believers have a role in sustaining fellow believers by intercessory prayer. This is the *means* of strength the Church has available to it. The *basis* of that confidence follows in the last part of the verse: ". . .the supply of the Spirit of Jesus

Christ." The Holy Spirit has been poured out upon all flesh (Acts 2). He has come to be a Helper, to provide supernatural assistance to the believer in the hour of crisis (John 14:16-18).

Facing the future, Paul assesses his role in life, his reason for existence. It is his desire that Christ should be glorified in him, whether it be by his living or his dying (v. 20). This is the center of his life—Christ is *everything* (v. 21). Paul understands the meaning of "lordship." He has surrendered all rights to himself. His *real* bonds are those he has gladly chosen—the cords of love that bind him to the Lord (v. 13). "For to me to live is Christ, and to die is gain" is a crisp summary of Paul's entire philosophy of life.

Now, Paul pauses to consider the alternatives (vv. 22-26). He knows that death is the end of his earthly mission. But, it is also the beginning of another and greater existence, in the very presence of his Lord! "Which is far better," Paul exclaims. Somehow, God has disclosed to Paul a little of the glory that awaits the believer. For Paul, death holds no terror. He can face this prospect with calm. Only the Christian believer can have this wonderful assurance!

And, Paul reports, the believer really has the best of *both* worlds. He knows that as long as the Lord gives him breath, God is not finished with him in this world. Paul is not certain of the outcome of his impending trial, but there is a buoyant note, an air of expectation. He does have the feeling that God has work for him yet to do and he will indeed be released. In fact, we know from sources other than Philippians that Paul *was* released and he spent up to 7 more years in a whirlwind of evangelistic endeavor, before passing on the torch to younger leaders (2 Timothy 4:6-8).

31

So, Paul is not despondent. Far from it! He is caught between two *delights*! (v. 23). He knows that leaving this world by the gates of death is *triumph* for the believer. But, until God says, "It is enough," there is plenty of work to do here.

What this passage really reports is that for the believer life has been given meaning and purpose. In a world desperately clawing for values and struggling for meaning, the Christian has a powerful message. As the century winds toward its close, more and more people are frightened about the prospects for the future. Paul charts the way for dealing with life's greatest difficulties. What a powerful, joyful word!

4

Loyal Citizens

READ PHILIPPIANS 1:27-30

Paul has just told the Philippians that as long as God gives him breath, he knows he has a purpose for living in this present world. He knows that at the end of life the Lord has reserved a wonderful existence for him. Heaven is the glorious hope of the believer in Jesus Christ!

But, in this little paragraph, Paul features the here-and-now dimension of the Christian's outlook. Here, he is not so much looking *ahead* as looking *around*. What is a Christian to do in this world? How is he to conduct himself? Illuminating, vivid figures of speech are used in this passage to convey Paul's point, the most significant being that of *citizenship*.

Citizens of Two Worlds

Verse 27 could be translated something like this: "Whatever happens, behave as good citizens worthy of the gospel of Christ." The figure of citizenship is highly appropriate for more than one reason. First, Paul is writing from Rome, the seat of world government, where citizenship was highly prized. And, he is writing to Philippi, a city given a special status in the empire as a virtual extension of the city of Rome itself. Citizens of Philippi prided themselves in their

33

role within the empire. So, the word would have great significance for his hearers.

In addition, the use of the word *citizen* (in verb form in this passage, not a noun) provides for Paul a means of expressing profound truths about the true nature of the Christian life. Paul sees the Christian as bearing a responsibility and enjoying the privileges of a *dual* citizenship. Occasionally Americans, by being born to American parents in a foreign land, are accorded the choice of selecting which country they wish to belong to, or, in some rare cases, they may maintain citizenship in both the United States and the other country.

Paul sees the Christian as being in this latter category. He is a citizen of this world by being born here. And, because of his *new birth*, he is a citizen of a heavenly realm! This analogy is prominent in Paul's writings. It appears again in Philippians in 3:20. In Ephesians, another of the Prison Epistles, it is a prominent concept. Even in the introduction to that Epistle, the strong implication is there: "To the saints which are at Ephesus [the visible, earthly realm], and to the faithful in Christ Jesus [the heavenly realm]" (Ephesians 1:1).

What Paul is saying in this initial clause in Philippians 1:27 is really: "Behave as a citizen of this world so as to authentically reflect your *real* citizenship in heaven." There may be two worlds, but there is no question about where the believer's highest loyalties lie! He is to exhibit Christ transparently to a broken world. He is the best kind of citizen of *both* worlds when he does this, although the world system may not be fully aware of this and may persecute the believer. The tension for the believer does not lie inside himself. Rather, it lies between

34

himself as a "two-world citizen" and the hostility to Christ and the kingdom of God that pervades this world.

Against the background of this passage is a reminder that "this world is not my home." Although there are beautiful sunsets to be enjoyed and marvelous delights set here by God for man, they have been discolored by the mark of sin. So, the believer holds the things of this world lightly, always remembering that his primary citizenship is not of this world, but of another—an invisible realm, that someday will become visible when the Lord himself shall appear!

Hold That Line!

In a football game, the stands may rock with the plea, "Hold that line," when the home team is being pushed across the field by the visiting team. The expression in verse 27 pictures the gladiator in the arena, faced with wild animals. The believer is likened to those condemned to fight for their lives. He may be tempted to back away from the forces of evil arrayed against him. But a mark of the true citizen of heaven is to "hold that line." He is not to flinch, waver, or give ground. He is to stand firm. Steadfastness is an important mark of a genuine believer.

This theme of steadfastness is an oft-repeated concept throughout Scripture. (See, for example: Matthew 10:22; 24:13; Revelation 2:26.) Those who begin the journey by faith are admonished to maintain that relationship. Incidentally, this emphasis on persistence, and perseverance undercuts the "eternal security" notion. The believer's security is conditioned by steadfast faith.

A United Front

The steadfastness of the Christian, featured in verse 27, is amplified in the expressions that follow: "I will know that you stand firm *in one spirit, contending as one man...*" *(NIV)*. This is describing how the believer is to engage in spiritual warfare. He does not act alone! The marvel of God's plan is that He has arranged for the spiritual battle to be fought by *clusters* of believers. These clusters are the churches scattered throughout the world, churches that are comprised of born-again believers, united in their faith and loyalty to Christ. The wonderful aspect of this united front is that when one member is assailed, there are others nearby who can rush to the aid of their beleaguered colleague.

It is possible that Paul had in mind a kind of armament employed in the service of Rome. In combat, those in the front ranks sometimes used large, interlocking shields, forming a solid wall against arrows and spears. This was called a *phalanx*. It was an extremely effective device.

When Christians spend their energies assaulting other believers, the devil must cheer. Dilution of the resources of God's people by bickering, faultfinding, and sabotage is a great and unnecessary hindrance to the work of God. Greatness of spirit lies in the ability to affirm one another in the family of God, and to rejoice when another receives advancement. Christian love ought to begin in the house of God.

Defending the Faith

What do you fight for? There is a time and a reason to fight, you know. The problem is that some Christians fight the wrong way and the wrong opponent! This is certainly not a plea for cultivating a contentious spirit. Christians ought not to be known for their belligerence. But, there are times when the Christian must not be afraid to stand up, even if it means risking hostility or even death. When the gospel is at stake, one's eternal life is involved. The good news of salvation in Jesus Christ cannot be negotiated away. Paul calls for courage, "contending as one man for the faith of the gospel" (v. 27, *NIV*).

Years ago, a teenager visited a Pentecostal church. There she heard about the baptism in the Holy Spirit. Her study of the Bible convinced her this message was true and she coveted the experience. Her father, however, was enraged. He forbade her ever to attend that humble church again. The girl was faced with a decision: should she obey her father, or should she obey the truth and risk the ill will of her father?

She was banished from home when she decided to continue attending the church. For several weeks she lived in the home of a godly Christian family. She had "contended for the faith." Eventually, her father realized the experience she had received had not ruined her, and he let her return home. The sequel to this story is that in the process of time, that young lady became a Pentecostal missionary and labored successfully for years in the Far East. She risked much for the truth.

Don't Be Afraid!

Paul continues his theme of steadfastness in verse 28. In picturing the proper attitude of Christians under fire, he employs a word that is unique in the New Testament. It is used in other literature to describe the stampeding of frightened horses.

37

"Don't allow yourself to be stampeded" might be an apt paraphrase of the passage.

Returning to the imagery of the arena, it seems as if Paul is picturing the beleaguered Christians being threatened by fierce enemies. Who were these enemies? At this point in Philippi, it is not likely they were the Roman authorities or the Jewish opposition, so common in other cities at that time. Rather, the Philippians were probably facing the threat of mob violence, of neighbors in the community who were angered by the Christian threat to their paganism. Whatever the opposition actually was, Paul is evidently aware that the possibility of violence lurks in Philippi. Against the advancing opposition, Paul urges his readers not to be terrified. A mark of Christian faith is indeed the ability to hold steady when others are losing their composure.

At a very low point during the Korean War, the American forces decided to invade the peninsula at a point far behind enemy lines. This famous Inchon landing became a turning point in that war. It was decided that several destroyers would be sent close to shore to draw enemy gunfire. This would expose the gun emplacements, permitting aircraft to bomb the positions; thus preparing for a more successful landing. The destroyers would be "sitting ducks." It was a suicide mission.

On board one of the destroyers, a band of born-again believers found comfort in regular prayer meetings. God gave them an unusual sense of peace. One could tell the Christians from the unbelievers simply by the facial expressions. The unbelievers were troubled; the Christians were serene—it was a startling contrast! And, in the end, in spite of hellish bombardment from Red tanks lined wheel to wheel on the beach, and heavy damage to the ships, not

one was sunk. And, aboard the ship with the praying men, no lives were lost! God heard the prayer of
these men and gave them peace and safety.

Two Signs

Paul exhorts the Philippians to view the tensions
with their neighbors as witnesses or *signs*. In the
gladiatorial ring, the crowd would signal their
pleasure or displeasure with the combatants, by calling for death or for mercy. Here, Paul pictures the
Christians in the arena receiving signals, but not
from the crowd. It is God himself who gives the
signs. And, these signs are not mere wishes; they
are statements of reality.

What is it that God signals through their
distresses? He gives a guarantee of the *destruction*
of those who are assailing the Christians and a
guarantee of the *salvation* of the believers. The surly
mob, blinded by sin, receives judgment. Courageous
Christians are made to know that ultimately, if not
now, they will receive the victor's wreath. Salvation
here does not guarantee exemption from suffering or
even death; it does guarantee the approval of God
and a home in heaven. Even the persecution through
which they may go is kept within the boundaries of
God's sovereign will. It will not destroy them!

The Gift of Suffering

Ours is called the "antiseptic society." We are
conditioned by heavy media bombardment to
believe that our happiness is totally dependent on
our using the right deodorant or toothpaste. At any
cost, our comfort must be secured. We avoid using
direct words to confront pain and loss. The funeral
home is now a mortuary. The funeral itself is called a

39

memorial service. Even within the church, contemporary material and moral values drawn from the world, continually press upon believers with alluring appeal. Ideas that are good in themselves, such as "positive thinking," are easily made into a rationalization for seeking security, comfort, and luxury. Against this modern-day pressure, how strange sound the words of Paul in Philippians 1:29: "For unto you it is given . . . to suffer for his sake."

Suffering—a badge of honor! Paul is not advocating a morbid *seeking* of pain and misfortune. No. He is reporting that persecution for the sake of Christ is to be expected, but it is not outside the knowledge of God. He may permit such suffering, but it becomes for the Christian an opportunity to see God at work! It is actually a mark of God's favor. Consider what the writer to the Hebrews says about the stresses God permits in the life of the believer (Hebrews 12:5-11).

An Example to Follow

It is one thing to have *sympathy* for someone enduring affliction. But to have *empathy* is to enter into the suffering, to wear the same shoes. Paul reports (v. 30), that the suffering he is experiencing in Rome is of the same order as that through which the Philippians are going—and, it is real suffering. The word translated "conflict" is the word from which we get "agony."

Paul reminds the Philippians that he has entered into their common bond in affliction *twice*. When he first carried the gospel to their city he was assaulted most unjustly. How could they forget those dramatic moments! They had witnessed the beating, the jailing, and, finally, the banishment from the city, had they not? Now, years later, word has filtered back to Philippi that Paul is imprisoned again, and for much the same reason as was his Philippian confinement.

Paul lets his friends know that, as far as he is concerned, what he has endured, and is even yet enduring, is the same fundamental conflict through which they are passing. The warmth of Paul's Christian experience flows through these words. He reports a joyful camaraderie. They, together, have been honored by God to share suffering on behalf of Christ. Out of the midst of the shadows beams a light. Joy in the darkness! Enduring hardship with patience is for Paul a certificate of the highest citizenship.

5

Follow the Leader

READ PHILIPPIANS 2:1-11

H. B. Garlock, for many years the field secretary for the Assemblies of God missions program in Africa, made a habit of traveling through the bush with national pastors. As he lived and worked with them, his values and his Christian example rubbed off on many of them.

One particular habit he had was to stop on the road to remove boulders he found along the way. Few would bother to do this, but Missionary Garlock did. When the national pastor with him would protest at the inconvenience, his response would be, "But we will be making the road easier for those who follow." Years later, travelers through that region could immediately identify the "disciples" of Garlock, for they too would stop the vehicle to remove the boulders.

Christ Jesus came into the world primarily to make atonement for the sins of mankind. In that sense, His life cannot be followed, for none but He could bear the sins of the world on Calvary. In truth, He came into the world to die, to die a redemptive death. However, there is much about the Lord Jesus that can be emulated by His disciples. His life, so beautifully portrayed in the Gospel narratives, becomes for us a model of excellence, a pattern by which to gauge the quality of our lives. Our Lord exhorted His disciples to follow Him (Matthew 8:22). Paul gives fresh emphasis to the concept of imitating the example of the Lord in a variety of places (see 1 Corinthians 11:1, for example). The Holy Spirit has been given to focus a light on the Lord Jesus so we may be able to follow our Leader (John 16:14).

Four Reasons for Following Jesus

Philippians 2:1 really picks up the thought introduced in 1:27. The intervening verses are almost parenthetical. Paul's concern is with the unity of believers within the household of faith. Philippians 2:1-11 is a powerful argument for humility of spirit as an important quality to be cultivated in interpersonal relationships, with a view to effecting harmony among fellow believers. The model for such behavior is the Lord Jesus himself. But, before featuring the strategic role of the Lord, Paul identifies the following four underlying reasons why divisiveness must be avoided in the Christian family.

First, "consolation in Christ." This term probably should be translated, "exhortation by, or about Christ." That is, Paul is saying to his readers: "Since the Lord has given a command about unity, you should take His word seriously." Possibly Paul is referring to John 17.

Second, "comfort of love." That is to say, within the context of brotherly consideration for one another, love provides a kind of constraint on behavior. Love leans toward harmony, not self-centeredness. Love definitely runs counter to "superstar" ego trips.

Third, "fellowship of the Spirit." Ephesians 4:3, 4

supports the concept that a mark of the Spirit's ministry is the production of harmony in the Body. Have you noticed in a public meeting saturated with the powerful presence of the Holy Spirit, how a great throng of God's people seem moved upon in unison, as if some unseen hand were plucking the strings of a heavenly harp? It is a manifestation of the New Testament understanding of the Church as the *body* (a totality working in harmony) of Christ.

Fourth, "bowels and mercies." This is a figure of speech that was more meaningful in the ancient Near East than it is today. It could better be translated as "tenderness and compassion" (*New International Version*). The idea is the outward expression of a deep, inner yearning of compassion and concern. Paul is saying that a mark of the true believer is a desire to reach out to those about him, with a view to ministering to their apparent needs. We might call this caring simply *kindness*. What an antidote for party spirit and pride!

Four Results of Obedience

Verse 2 is an imperative: "Fulfill ye my joy." The strong implication of this verse is: "Please obey my appeal to you for harmony and humility." What results from this? Paul enumerates four things.

Paul intends that the Philippian Christians should be "like-minded." That is, they should be of the *same mind*. This is the desired and intended result of their willingness to serve one another in humility.

They are to expect "the same love." There is a clear emphasis here on the *mutual affection* that an open-hearted fellowship will produce.

"Being of one accord" means "of a *single spirit*."

No divided loyalties here. No dilution of interest or purpose. They are one in their whole outlook.

Finally, "of *one mind*." This is really a repetition of the first item in this list. By repeating this, as the first and last elements in his catalog, Paul is emphasizing the concept of the unity of the Body. Division is a cardinal sin among the members of the body of Christ.

Lowliness of Mind

Pride comes in two forms: one may think too highly of himself (Romans 12:3), or he may *depreciate* himself. Picture the pastor or Sunday school superintendent asking someone in the church to teach a class. "Oh, I could never do that!" is a common response. However, upon examination, one may discover that the individual being approached for the job was really hungering for an ego-inflating word. "Sure, George, I know you can do it!" That craving for reinforcement, marked by the declining of the initial invitation, really may betray a kind of false humility. Another word for it is pride.

In verse 3, Paul is appealing, not for a feigned humility, but for an honest appraisal and a genuine appreciation of the abilities and talents of others. This does not have to be self-deprecating; rather, it looks *outward*. It is an attitude that is quick to encourage one's colleagues. This attitude absolutely stifles the possibility of "strife." This outward-looking stance is caught beautifully in verse 4. This attitude is truly a Christlike virtue. The same root word for "lowliness" is found in this passage, as well as in Matthew 11:29, where it refers directly to the Lord Jesus himself.

An Early Hymn

In the Early Church, the believers "sang their faith." There are several outstanding examples of hymns that are quoted by the writers of the New Testament. These hymns are packed with doctrine, leading some to conclude that they were possibly creeds; some of which, at least, were set to a pleasing rhythm and probably sung at public worship.

One of the best examples of such an early hymn is Philippians 2:5-11. This beautiful set of metrical verses glorifies the Lord for His willingness to lay aside the splendor of heaven, which was rightfully His. He came to our world, and here suffered the greatest of humiliations on our behalf. The background for this hymn is obviously Isaiah 52 and 53, in which the Lord is pictured as coming first as the "suffering Servant," before He comes in triumph and glory. There is also in this hymn a strong contrast between the first Adam, who arrogantly desired to have that which was forbidden to him in the Garden of Eden, and the Lord, the Second Adam, who willingly laid aside what was rightfully His.

Before examining this hymn more closely, let us make this observation. The New Testament is not written as if it were a "handbook on theology." No, it is not a catalog of sterile items. In fact, much of the doctrine taught in the New Testament is "tucked in" almost inconspicuously. Paul, for example, deals with real, practical problems of daily life in the lives of the earliest Christians and in the young churches. In solving their problems, Paul brings in at various points profound spiritual truths.

In the passage at hand, Paul is trying to teach the Philippians the importance of humility, as a vital

Christian virtue. How does he accomplish his purpose? He points to Christ. He quotes a hymn that probably was familiar to the Philippians, or was known to Paul in Rome. And, in the process, we are blessed with some of the most impressive teaching in the Bible about the person and work of Christ.

The Preincarnate Christ

So, Paul admonishes his readers to have the same mind-set as the Great Leader himself, the Lord Jesus Christ (v.5). "Follow the leader," Paul exhorts.

The hymn really begins with verse 6. Here the Lord is pictured before His incarnation. He was the Second Person of the Trinity from before the beginning of time. He is in the "form" of God himself. This is a way of saying that He is God, equal with the Father and having the attributes of Deity in every respect. The "glory" of God was His by right! It was not an act of robbery for Him to express that glory. Notice here the obvious contrast to the first Adam, whose attempt to be like the gods (Genesis 3) was an act of robbery.

Jesus Christ stood outside of time and space before the Incarnation. In fact, numerous passages link the Lord Jesus with the act of creation of all that is. (See, for example: John 1, Colossians 1, and Hebrews 1.) Here is majesty and power! Here is splendor and glory unsurpassed! And it is all His by right!

Incarnation

Verse 7 compresses into a few words the colossal truth of the Incarnation. Here is the result of the choice that Christ made before time began. His self-

47

denial led Him from the glory that was His by right to laying aside for a time the expression of that glory. No, He did not "lose" His deity in the process; He simply chose not to express it openly, except on special occasions. (See Matthew 17:1-13, for example.) He "emptied" himself of the glory of heaven, or as the Authorized Version says: "[He] made himself of no reputation."

In that "emptying," the Lord took upon himself the form of a servant (literally, a "slave," one with no rights). He was made in the likeness of man, identifying with all the pain, feelings, and sufferings that are part of our human existence. Jesus, in coming into this world, participated deeply and fully in all that it means to be human. This is what allows us to call Him the God-man; fully God and fully man. Never has there been anyone like this in all of human history!

Obedient Unto Death

Jesus did not come into this world as a fullgrown adult; He was born as a tiny infant. And, He did not come into a wealthy home with riches and power. He came into a humble family and was born in the humblest of circumstances (Luke 2). He was reared in a dusty village, a crossroads of commercial life, Nazareth—which must have been filled with the noises and odors of caravan traffic. He lived in the rough-and-tumble everyday world common to the ordinary people of all ages.

Verse 8 carries us swiftly on to the culmination of the life of our Lord. As the Gospels faithfully record, Jesus was arrested in an unjust manner; He was tried before prejudiced judges—a mockery of the law. Humiliated, beaten, and condemned to a common criminal's death—in all this Jesus did not attempt to retaliate. He bore the indignity and the shame quietly, obediently. He recognized that it was not for Him to evade the cross. It was for this reason He had come into the world!

The Cross! It was a shame for a Jew to "hang on a tree"; it was the meanest of deaths the Romans could inflict. At Calvary, Jesus suffered the most humiliating of deaths in either culture. He tasted death for every man (Hebrews 2:9). His obedience made our deliverance possible. What a marvel—that out of death comes forth life! Here is the magnificent example of self-giving love. Here is Greatness stooping to the lowest. This is the noblest story ever told. Can you understand why Paul would put this great hymn regarding the incarnation of the Lord into a practical passage exhorting humility and consideration for others? There is no loftier Example available!

Triumph!

How wonderful that the story does not end with verse 8! There is a sequel to the tale just told: "Wherefore God also hath highly exalted him. . . ." The atonement has been completed. The scene changes. And here, condensed into a single expression, is the high drama of the events the Gospel writers carefully record. On the third day after that cruel death, Jesus rose from the dead, fulfilling His own prophecies. The Resurrection is a guarantee that the sacrificial death of Jesus was effective. How the Early Church shouted the good news! The Lord is risen (1 Corinthians 15)!

And, He is ascended! Forty days after His resurrection, Jesus was taken from among His followers (Acts 1). His work on earth was finished. He had paid for the sins of the whole world. He had lived an exemplary life among men. He had risen from the dead; displaying to the universe that His death had achieved its purpose. Now He was returning to the glory that was His by right! Seated at the right hand of the Father, Jesus now fulfills His role as High Priest, Intercessor, bearing the needs of His followers (Hebrews 1:3).

What's in a name? In our culture, we look over lists of names and, as parents, select a name that sounds pleasant to us. Not so in the ancient Near East. A name held great significance. It was a virtual extension of the personality of the person named. It represented the character of the individual. And this is true in the case of our Lord himself. In verses 10 and 11, the hymn conveys this idea. The name of Jesus is above every name. There is no authority greater than this!

All things are not yet under the final dominion of the Lord. That day has not fully come, but the final victory has been assured by His successful death and resurrection. The devil has already been defeated. He is engaged in "guerrilla warfare," with no hope of winning in the end. The devil may appear to be winning on many fronts today, but he is a beaten foe! The day will come when every being in the universe will acknowledge Christ as Lord of all. Those who commit their lives to Him *now* will reign with Him then. Those who oppose Him now will bow their knees *then*, but it will be too late. Every voice in the universe will cry out that Jesus Christ is Lord. Believers will acknowledge Him with joy. Unbelievers will acknowledge Him with sorrow and remorse. This is encouragement to look to Jesus *now*. "Following the Leader" is wisdom and safety.

6

Christianity in Jeans

READ PHILIPPIANS 2:12-18

Christianity in jeans? Yes, that's right! In the previous chapter, we considered the lofty example of the Lord himself in His obedience and self-giving humility. The hymn recorded in the paragraph in Philippians just preceding verses 12-18 elevates the vision of the reader to the highest heights, soaring to eternity past and sweeping to eternity future. It is a cosmic view, indeed!

From this breathtaking panorama, Paul changes the scene abruptly. He turns from the heavenly view to the earthly scene. He shifts from portraying Christ in His matchless splendor to examining how we, mere mortals, are to behave. Paul wants us to see that the message of the Cross is relevant and applicable to daily life.

Obedience Required

"Wherefore" ties together this section of the Book with the previous passage. Here, Paul makes his appeal, based on the shining example of the Lord Jesus Christ. The appeal is for obedience. Paul is not scolding the Philippians. He is not rebuking them for gross neglect. Not at all. In fact, the tone of the passage is one of warmth and appreciation. "My beloved friends," he calls them. And, in his exhortation to obedience, he is quick to emphasize that he is aware they have been characterized by obedient behavior since he has known them. It is a way of life with them. His admonition, then, is to call attention to the importance of an obedient spirit in the life of the Christian, while encouraging them to *continue* in that path.

Obedience to what, or to whom? The context of the passage is clear. Their ultimate allegiance is to the Lord Jesus Christ. Just as the Lord was obedient to His Heavenly Father, so believers are urged to submit to the demands of Christ upon them. How are they to know what the Lord wants? This was the ministry of the apostles. Commissioned by Christ himself, the apostles were instruments of the Holy Spirit to speak the will of God to His people.

The Bible becomes for us the principal means by which we learn how the Lord would have us to live day by day. The Holy Spirit takes the written Word, convincing believers of its truth, and points us to the Living Word. Our task is to come to the Word of God, sincerely wanting to hear what God desires of us and willing to obey His will with eager delight. The mark of the believer, then, is eagerness to obey.

Paul is pleased with the Philippians. When he was with them during the brief visits he made to their city, he was impressed with their willingness to obey. Now, in his absence, Paul wants them to continue to have this attitude. It is like a foreman on the job who steps out on an errand. He wants to know that the crew who have been faithfully discharging their responsibilities while he is watching them will do the same while he is gone. Paul expects this of the Philippians. He is not assuming anything less of them.

Incidentally, isn't this generally a good practice in

dealing with your colleagues and friends? *Assume the best*, and you are likely to be rewarded with positive results. Assuming the worst frequently turns out to be a self-fulfilling prophecy!

Work Out Your Salvation

How frequently this passage has been twisted! Some would gather from this expression in verse 12 that our salvation depends on us alone; that somehow we keep ourselves saved. This is at best only a partial picture of the full story. This verse might better be translated: "Work out what Christ has worked in"; or, "Get working with your salvation." No, we don't "work" to get saved or stay saved (Ephesians 2:8, 9).

What Paul is talking about here has nothing to do with the security of the believer. Rather, he is talking about the characteristic life-style appropriate to believers. How should a Christian live? The setting is not the individual Christian, but the Christian as he lives and works together in a community of faith. It is a picture of a local Christian church and how its members are to relate to one another and to the world to witness to the redeeming power of the Lord. They are to have their eyes on the well-being of each other, emulating the humble and loving example of the Lord.

How are the Philippians to "work out" what Christ has "worked in" them? The proper perspective is "fear and trembling." Paul uses this same expression in 2 Corinthians 7:15 and Ephesians 6:5; in each case, picturing the believer relying, not on his own strength, but humbly trusting in the Lord. It is not intended, then, to convey the idea of terror—lest one be cast into hell, losing his salvation. It is expressed here to show that our proper relationship to one another in the family of God, the sphere of our Christian living, can be exercised only in the power of the Lord. Our strength and wisdom are not adequate for this task.

The Enabling

God has provided the gift of salvation for us. He wants that gift to "percolate" through our lives, affecting all our relationships. The change in the way the believer lives ought to point to the One who wrought the change. Obedience is the way the new life in Christ is nourished and exercised. It is our part in the divine-human cooperation to give place to the Holy Spirit (Galatians 5:16-18). Making room for the power of God is our main task. Obedience to the Lord is an important means of cultivating the working of God in our lives. Failure to obey grieves the Holy Spirit. The Lord expressed this simple truth profoundly: "If ye love me, keep my commandments" (John 14:15).

Verse 13 focuses full attention on God's activity. It is cast in terms of an explanation of Paul's main intent. "Get working with your salvation." Why? "For it is God. . . ." God at work! The word used for "work" here is "energizing" or "enabling." God is effective in what He does.

A breathtaking statement is tucked into this passage. God enables, not only in the "doing," but also in supplying the "willing." Those who open their lives to the Lord discover their *desires* are increasingly conformed to the divine desire. Our minds are in the process of a continual transformation (Romans 12:2). It is His "good pleasure" to do this for us!

Verse 14 is a direct, unqualified appeal. "Do *everything*. . . ." That takes in the whole ball park. And what he asks of the Philippians is a "mind stopper"! *No complaining. No arguing.* "But, Lord, You know there are *some* things that everybody has a right to grumble about!" Paul does not allow for these little loopholes. What is he really saying?

Isn't Paul asking that the Philippians cultivate such transparent faith in the Lord that they are willing to trust Him with *all* their needs? This does not mean they are to be *naive*. Surely there are inequities and injustices of which they must be aware. They are not asked to stumble blindly through life. No. But they are asked to behave in their circumstances in a *positive* and constructive way. They must not go about with a sour attitude, sniping at all the things around them that are unlovely. Because they are in Christ, they can see every problem as an opportunity to observe God at work. Life's difficulties become opportunities to demonstrate faith. The Christian is to be buoyant and hopeful. He has, after all, an inner strength that this world knows nothing of!

The result of such positive living is described in verse 15: "That ye may be blameless and harmless, the sons of God, without rebuke."

Blameless. This means they are to live such a life that no one could have reason to accuse them of wrongdoing. That's a high expectation!

Harmless. This word was used in Roman times to describe wine that was not diluted with water, or metal that was unmixed with materials that would weaken it. The word, then, means "pure" or "simple." Believers are to be known for straightforward, transparent behavior, not deviousness or craftiness. The Christian is to live so that the Lord for whom he is an ambassador will be exalted and not hurt. The ethical behavior of Christians to each other and toward the world is an important part of our witness (Romans 12:17).

Sons of God. The contrast between the Christian's style of life and that of the children of this world is Paul's intended point. Just as the soldier at the time of Christ's crucifixion exclaimed: "Truly this was the Son of God" (Matthew 27:54), so Paul expects the believers in Philippi to be models, as well. His expectation is that their neighbors and friends will see Christ in their lives.

The Old Testament phraseology, "a crooked and perverse generation," repeated in Deuteronomy 32:5 and in Psalm 78:8, is employed here to describe the surrounding community in which the Christian family is to live and work. We sing, "This world is not my home." Paul spells it out here. We are strangers in a strange land, a land not friendly to the Lord. This is realism. This is facing things as they really are.

Bright Stars in a Dark Night

How is the Christian to understand his proper role, then, if he is faced with the grim fact of living in a hostile environment? The last part of verse 15 expresses it imaginatively: "Shine as lights in the world." Have you ever looked at the stars on a still, clear night—pinpoints of light in a vast darkness? What an accurate picture of the Christian in an alien world! The darkness does not overwhelm the light. Not at all! In fact, the darker the night, the more brilliant the stars appear. This is no picture of defeat and dejection. It is a call to hope, to action, to triumph!

Verse 16 really belongs to the preceding verse. The expression "holding forth the word of life" describes the call to shine as stars. To exhibit Christ, the Word of Life, is the way the Christian is going to best move against the darkness of this world. His life and his voice are to lift up the risen Lord. There is no message to compare with the good news! Jesus is the light that shined into the darkness (John 1:7-9). Our task is to reflect that Light, just as the moon reflects the light of the sun. Lifting up Christ is our mission.

Paul's Testimony

The scene shifts. Paul has been looking at the example of Christ and exhorting the Philippians. Now, in the latter part of Philippians 2:16, Paul turns to his own story. He expresses his personal feelings, aspirations, and experiences.

Picture a Roman stadium. The runners are on the track; the crowd is cheering and waving. At the end of the race, the winner is awarded the wreath of leaves and the applause of the crowd. It is this athletic allusion that forms the setting for Paul's testimony. He pictures himself as one who has been running a race. His winning is not dependent on his efforts alone. *This* race, of which he speaks, is to be won by a relay. His achievement is dependent on the behavior and performance of his Christian converts; they are his testimony. Their lives are his trophies.

This analogy is picked up again in Philippians 4:1. It is a common word picture throughout Paul's writings. His plea, then, is that the Philippians continue to exhibit the marks of genuine

57

Christianity faithfully to the end, so that at the great day of accounting, he will not be found to have run his race in vain. But great will be his reward to see the fruit of his labors on that day.

Now the metaphor changes. Verse 17 takes us from the stadium to the temple. Every Roman community had not only stadiums, but also amphitheaters and, especially, temples, as necessary public buildings for their pattern of life. Images drawn from athletics, from the marketplace, and from the ritual of worship, therefore, were common enough to be useful in communicating important ideas.

Paul pictures himself here as being offered on a sacrificial altar. It is in the present tense. He is doubtless referring to his confinement, and to the imminent trial on which his life depends. He is facing the end of life. In a real sense, his life is being offered up. The literal pouring out of his blood may become a grisly reality, much as a drink offering might be poured out in the temple.

Important here is that Paul links his possible execution with the "service and faith" of the Philippians. Their faithfully standing with him for Christ is intimately linked with his own sacrifice. They share together in each other's witness and in one another's needs.

Paul is thinking of their kindness in sending Epaphroditus with a love gift from them to Rome. He is linking his life with theirs. Paul does not stand apart from them, as if his sacrifice and witness were superior to theirs. No, they are together. Although the world may oppose them and cause them suffering and heartache, they endure patiently, knowing it is a worthy race that is being run.

Joy

Paul faces the possibility of death with joy! He shares his joy with the Philippians. No trial or stress, not even the prospect of a violent death, can tarnish the joy he expresses. Christ transforms suffering. Especially, when it is shared with like-minded friends who love the Lord.

7

Highest Honors

READ PHILIPPIANS 2:19-30

It is graduation time. Distinguished guests grace the platform. The auditorium is filled with parents and friends. But the focus of attention is on the honored graduates, struggling with unfamiliar and awkward caps and gowns. As the graduates eventually pass in review to receive their diplomas, a handful are given special recognition. Some graduate with honor (*cum laude*). A small number are accorded high honors (*magna cum laude*). But, the ovations of the assembled guests go to that very small group who graduate with *highest honors (summa cum laude)*. These are rewarded by public acclaim for years of hard work and superior achievement.

In the Christian realm, we sometimes fail to acknowledge worthy colleagues. And, when we do, it is not always for the kinds of reasons especially called for in the Scriptures. It is proper, surely, to recognize the academic achievements of outstanding high school or college students who attend Christian churches. It is not improper to give trophies to winning church baseball teams, winning Bible quiz teams, or outstanding competitors in musical talent. We honor those around us who demonstrate various kinds of success. This is not out of order. It is good to promote worthy endeavors. But, it is much more difficult to single out *faithfulness* and *compassion* and *self-sacrifice*. Some of the noblest qualities of life are not easily measured from an earthly perspective.

Even if we miss some of the greatest among us in this fashion, it is nevertheless important to reflect on what true greatness is. And we must not be diverted from giving whatever emphasis may be possible to these intangible, immeasurable qualities. This is the importance of the passage at hand. Paul pauses to consider those about him who are worthy of highest honor. He cites *two* for *summa cum laude* recognition in Christian service.

A Trip Planned

Paul is caught between two possibilities. He is not certain whether the trial he awaits will result in his release or his death. Throughout this entire passage, his uncertainty is reflected. In verse 19, however, the pendulum swings in the direction of an expectation of release from imprisonment. Paul wants to send Timothy, who is with him in Rome (Philippians 1:1), to Philippi immediately. His purpose is that in place of his own personal visit, Timothy will bear greetings on his behalf to them and be a blessing to them. Paul also expects Timothy to return with good news from Philippi; thus blessing Paul in return.

Paul has been discussing his own aspirations (vv. 16-18). Now his attention shifts to the role of two of his colleagues: Timothy, who has been with him in his Roman imprisonment, and Epaphroditus, who is a leader in the church at Philippi. His purpose is to point out the qualities of service both of these men exhibit. They are worthy examples of Christian living that all the readers would do well to emulate.

Christ is the supreme model. But Paul recognizes that there are some mere mortals with whom his readers can readily identify as outstanding illustrations of Christlikeness. Timothy, the first of these, Paul holds up to the Philippians as a model of excellence. He wants the Philippians, on his arrival in their city, to receive him and honor him as a paragon of Christian virtue. His life is to be read like a "living epistle."

A Sad Contrast

Verse 20 is the loftiest praise Paul gives to any man. Of all his colleagues, particularly the Christian leaders in the vicinity of Rome, there is none who is "like-minded." That is, none shares so deeply Paul's passion for ministry, his sacrificial giving of himself for the cause of Christ and for others. Paul promises that when Timothy arrives in Philippi, he will "care for your state." How? "Naturally." That is, his love for the Lord has so developed that the Christlike quality of self-giving love is "natural" to him. It is not an act to be put on; it is not like a robe he can take off. Timothy is genuine in his service from the inside out!

What a contrast to the others laboring in the gospel! Verse 21 is painful. It carries us back to Philippians 1:15 and 16. There were, to be sure, ministers in Rome who were "huckstering the gospel," not really living up to the highest level of Christian maturity. They were divided in mind. They proclaimed the gospel of saving faith in Christ and likely saw converts drawn to the Lord. But, in their personal lives, they had an uneven development. Self-seeking, jealousy, envy, and other unlovely qualities yet remained to be sloughed off.

No, God does not wait until people are perfect before He uses them! This does not condone or excuse disappointing, even sinful, behavior. It does remind us, however, that our eyes must be raised to the highest models. Christ is to be the object of our attention, not the misdeeds of men. When we do find good examples, we should not, however, be fearful of reporting, "Here is what I mean. Here is an example of Christ."

An Unlikely Candidate

Timothy was known to the Philippians. He had been with Paul on the second journey when the church had been established. The Philippians knew a special relationship existed between Paul and this young man, a father-son relationship. By this, Paul meant that Timothy was "his own son in the faith" (1 Timothy 1:2). It was on the first journey into Asia Minor, when Paul visited Lystra, that Timothy had been led to the Lord. Not many years later, on the second journey, Paul asked this lad to join him as a kind of understudy on his tour across the Mediterranean world (Acts 16:1).

What kind of man was Timothy? His mother was Jewish; his father a Greek. We know nothing of his father. This absence of information leads to the conjecture that there was a division in the home about spiritual matters. It was not an ideal background. What a comfort to young people who fear they may never amount to much because they come from a broken home! Timothy is a good example of one who survived unpleasant circumstances.

Timothy was not robust physically or emotionally. Paul sent him on limited assignments at first. Gradually, he sent him on more demanding missions. But, throughout Paul's references to him, there is a note of concern. He is asked to take care of his gastrointestinal problems (1 Timothy 5:23). Paul admonishes the Corinthian church not to frighten the young man (1 Corinthians 16:10), and he urges Timothy to be encouraged (1 Timothy 4:12). These are all evidences that Timothy needed special support and encouragement. The picture one gets from all this is of a young man with less than an ideal background, who was physically frail and somewhat retiring in disposition. Hardly an impressive leader! Yet, Paul recognizes that God's hand is on Timothy. He is an instrument of the Lord.

Is it possible that Timothy's awareness of his limitations helped him to trust that much more in the Lord? Certainly his spirit is a model of excellence. His self-sacrificing love is known to the Philippians. And Paul presents him as a model of Christian values that they would do well to remember and imitate.

As soon as Paul learns the outcome of the trial (v. 23), he plans to send Timothy to Philippi. Paul also hopes to make the trip to Philippi himself. In the meantime, this letter of tribute, with the highest honor Paul accords any of his colleagues, will precede Timothy.

One of Their Own

The name *Epaphroditus* means "charming." Chosen to represent the Philippians in their mission of mercy to Paul, Epaphroditus had journeyed to Rome. But en route or after his arrival, he became desperately ill, almost to the point of death. Now, upon his recovery, he is returning to Philippi, and Paul uses this occasion to send a "thank-you letter" to the church. Verse 25 contains a veritable catalog of commendations for Epaphroditus. Paul has a towering estimate of the quality and worth of this man.

My brother. Paul warmly identifies with Epaphroditus as a fellow believer. He knew him in Philippi. Perhaps Paul had even led him to the Lord. It is fitting that his recognition of him as a Christian brother is at the top of his list.

Companion in labor. Is it possible in the brief time Paul had spent in Philippi that Epaphroditus and Paul had worked together in the gospel? We can only speculate as to what specific sphere of Christian service Paul is referring to, but he acknowledges that they have worked together in some capacity furthering the gospel of Christ.

Fellow soldier. Here is a clear allusion to "spiritual combat." They have both been under fire. They have been the targets of pressure from the Philippian pagan community, and now, in Rome, they are under the growing shadow of Roman suspicion. In the heat of battle one appreciates courageous comrades.

Your messenger. Literally, Epaphroditus has been the "apostle" of the Philippians. He is rendering a valuable service as the ambassador of that church, commissioned to be their representative. He not only carried the money of the Philippians with him, but also ministered to Paul in a variety of ways on their behalf.

He that ministered to my wants. The word translated "ministered" here comes from the concept of sacred, public service. Epaphroditus is credited with "ministry" in a special sense. It

carries the idea of actions rendered not only for
Paul's benefit, but also as an act of service and
worship to the Lord himself!

Compassion

Have you ever visited a patient in the hospital,
expecting to cheer him up, only to find that *you*
came away cheered by the patient? There are
delightful people in the household of faith who are
never preoccupied with their own needs, but are
continually thinking of others. Such a person was
Epaphroditus. Verse 26 tells the story.

Epaphroditus is described by two significant
words. "He *longed* after you all." Here is an
expression of intense feeling and deep yearning. It
describes a depth of profound attachment, a genuine
love. And, that love is marked by *heaviness*. This is
the same word used to describe the Lord's agony in
the Garden (Matthew 26:37). Deep mental and
spiritual anguish affected Epaphroditus because the
Philippians had heard that he was ill. There is no
concern for his own illness expressed here. Paul is
impressed with the deep compassion Epaphroditus
felt for his fellow Philippians. What a picture of
Christlike compassion!

Illness

Epaphroditus had been sick—very, very sick. Paul
reports in verse 27 just how sick he had really been.
He had recovered by the time Paul wrote this letter,
but he had been "nigh unto death." We do not know
the nature of the illness. What is more important is
that God intervened. He was delivered. Paul
describes this wonderful deliverance as an act of
God's mercy. This merciful deliverance had a double

blessing. Paul appreciates that it was in fact a blessing for Epaphroditus. But he has such a warm regard for him that he also sees his recovery as a mercy to Paul.

Paul was human. He was subject to depression. Evidently his discouragement was profound at the very time Epaphroditus was near death. Paul needed this good friend at that hour, perhaps more than at any other time. He needed special support. How merciful of God to spare his friend. God is faithful; He will not permit us to undergo stress beyond that which we can adequately handle (1 Corinthians 10:13).

A Life Risker

The Philippians are to receive their colleague Epaphroditus with joy. Paul is sending him back "the more carefully." Actually, this should be translated, "the more eagerly." Paul wants them to be reunited with their ambassador, Epaphroditus. Then they can receive their good friend with joy, knowing he has fulfilled his mission successfully and his illness was not fatal. Paul tells us, in verse 28, that the knowledge of such a happy reunion will not only make the Philippians and Epaphroditus joyful, but will also relieve Paul's sorrow.

Now, Paul explains how the Philippians are to receive their representative upon his return. "Receive him with all gladness, just as the Lord would receive him," would be a good way to translate this passage. They are not only to receive him *joyfully*, but are also to accord him the *highest honor*. He is to be awarded the *summa cum laude*. His courage and faithfulness in the face of harrowing trials are to be held aloft as a worthy model to tell the children about. Here is the finest kind of Christian character in action.

Why is this so? A term used to describe what Epaphroditus had accomplished is drawn from the burial customs of that day. Although not knowing the germ theory of disease, ancient peoples knew that those who buried the dead, especially in times of plague, subjected themselves to the risk of death itself. So it was with Epaphroditus. He was indeed a "life risker." He was worthy of honor!

8

Empty Expectations

READ PHILIPPIANS 3:1-6

How many times have you heard a preacher say, "Now, in conclusion...," only to go on speaking on a new point for a considerable time? Paul does this in Philippians 3. He indicates that he is about to close the letter (v. 1), but then goes into a series of extensive new ideas, before *really* concluding in 4:8.

Here in this "preliminary" conclusion, Paul issues several fatherly exhortations to his dear friends in Philippi, warning them about the dangers that lurk in the shadows. From this series of admonitions he drifts into a personal reminiscence. As he reflects on what God has done in his life, a flood of fresh thoughts pour onto the pages, causing him to forget his intention to conclude the letter. We can be grateful for these added comments in these chapters. Profound insights into the Christian experience are shared with us here.

Rejoice!

The most characteristic word for the entire Book of Philippians is *rejoice*. Nine times, in one form or other, this word occurs. It captures the spirit, the very essence, of Paul's message. Considering the difficulty through which Paul had come, and the trials and anguish the Philippians had encountered, this is a remarkable challenge.

The joy Paul speaks of is not a matter of wishful thinking or self-hypnosis. It is not merely an exercise in "positive thinking." The joy Paul talks about is a reality grounded in the nature of God and the fact of Christ's finished work. It is a reality that is made available to Christians through the ministry of the indwelling Holy Spirit. It is a solid dimension of Christian experience that is not dependent on outward circumstances. It is not a superficial smile. It can be "joy through tears." It is Paul's way of saying: "Set your face into the wind, into the teeth of the storm. Look life head on. Have confidence in the Lord. He will carry you through *anything*! Just watch God work!"

What a view of life! What a buoyancy it pictures. Deep, abiding joy—this is the powerful testimony of the child of God. It is a witness to a strong faith in the victorious Lord.

Concern for Your Welfare

Unlike some of the other New Testament churches, the Philippian church was not plagued with a host of problems. Heresy or moral entanglements did not hang heavy over this delightful congregation. They were a community of believers marked by obedience, compassion, and missionary vision—an ideal church. In fact, the only specific problem Paul addresses is the friction between two women in the church (Philippians 4:2). He admonishes them to settle their quarrel. But this problem does not compare in magnitude to the massive issues shaking the Galatian and Corinthian churches.

Even here, though, Paul in his fatherly concern recognizes that *safety* (v. 1) lies in awareness and vigilance. There are dark clouds that could in time break upon this delightful church. Paul is preparing them for what *could* happen in Philippi. They are not immune to dissension, heresy, or moral failure.

So, Paul reports to his readers that he feels it is important to repeat some matters for their welfare. For Paul to go over the cautions he feels they need to have reinforced, "is not grievous" for him. Actually, this could be translated, "It is no problem for me to do this."

Beware of Dogs

Verse 2 contains a sudden change of tone. From an appeal to rejoice, Paul turns to a sharp warning about impending danger. Three times in this verse he repeats, "Beware. . . ." What is it the Philippians are to guard against? Certainly it is not an immediate and present danger. But, Paul is obviously apprehensive about the future possibility of a serious problem affecting the Philippian church. The way the passage is constructed it is clear that the three-fold warning is really a compound warning about a *single* grave threat. What was this threat?

Dogs. In the Jewish world, dogs were regarded as the most miserable of creatures. In our society, we tend to think of dogs as lovable house pets, "man's best friend." But in the ancient Near East, and in much of the non-Western world of our day, dogs are considered useful only as street scavengers. The Jews of Jesus' day considered gentiles to be dogs—despised and unworthy. Here, in this verse, Paul turns the table over! Those he calls "dogs" are, without doubt, Judaizers! These Jewish Christians would go into a predominantly gentile church and coerce the congregation to adopt Jewish customs

71

and law. Although there probably weren't many Judaizers present at that moment in Philippi, they weren't far away, and they were obviously considered as prone to stirring up trouble.

Paul was still smarting from the problems caused by such traveling troublemakers. Upon his departure from Philippi during the second missionary journey, when the church there had been established, he had gone to Thessalonica and then on to Beroea. But a mob of Jews had followed him to Beroea from Thessalonica, and disrupted his efforts there (Acts 17:13).

Now, not all the Jews were Judaizers. Only those who had come into the Christian faith and had mixed Christian values with Jewish tradition could be called Judaizers. Wherever they came from, and whoever they were, Paul looked on their teachings as a serious threat to the purity of the gospel. The entire Book of Galatians addresses this critical problem; the most serious problem in the early years of the Church. It is no wonder that Paul wanted to protect the fledgling church in Philippi from any possible infiltration by this dangerous influence.

Paul adds a second criticism to these Judaizers. *Evil workers*, he calls them. A wry bit of irony is employed here. The Judaizers insisted on "works" as a way to salvation. Paul spurns their evil emphasis on "works."

Now, the final barb. *Concision* could be just as easily translated *mutilation*. It is an obvious reference to the Jewish practice of circumcision, a rite prescribed for all Jewish males. It is clearly a cultural custom, not required for salvation. This issue was settled at the great Jerusalem Council a decade before Paul wrote to the Philippians (Acts 15). Even before that, however, Paul had issued the

"Emancipation Proclamation" of the Christian gospel in the great letter to the Galatians. Gentiles need not undergo Jewish circumcision. In fact, the insistence that a gentile go through the Jewish patterns is considered by Paul to be a denial of faith in Christ. You can't have it both ways. You must trust in Christ completely—or not at all!

So serious is the matter that Paul likens the "cutting" of the Judaizers to the frenzied mutilations common in the local mystery cults of their day. The fanatical priests of these cults were known to slash themselves with knives during their religious rituals. Paul paints a vivid picture! He makes his point quite clear. Beware: mad dogs!

True Circumcision

Paul testifies to the reality of his own Christian experience. "We are the circumcision," he reports. He includes the Philippian readers, nearly all of whom are gentiles, in his sweeping statement. For Paul, true circumcision is of the heart (Romans 2:28, 29). The new Israel is comprised of Jew and gentile (Ephesians 2:11-22). A true relationship with God is a matter of spiritual life, not empty ritual. It does not depend on ethnic origin. Three statements are packed into verse 3 to emphasize this important truth.

Worship God in the spirit. Or, better, ". . . by the Spirit." The Holy Spirit has been given to us to enable us to worship the Lord truly (John 4:23, 24). When the Holy Spirit controls one's life, Christ is exalted (John 16:14). Here is a means of spiritual relationship far transcending the outward forms of Jewish legalism.

Rejoice in Christ Jesus. Really, it should be translated "boast," "glory," or "exalt." This is a

73

favorite Pauline term, expressing a very strong feeling. He is obviously contrasting this with the boasting of the Judaizers who prided themselves in their self-righteous performance. Paul calls on the believer to bask in the glory of the finished work of Christ. The essence of sin is prideful boasting, the veritable enthronement of self. The kind of "glorying" Paul repeatedly invites the Christian to is a call to humility of self, giving all the glory to the Lord.

Confidence in the flesh. This is the key issue of the entire passage. With revulsion, Paul turns from all false confidence. To place confidence in anything outside Christ, any personal achievement, is to have confidence in "the flesh." Paul pulls away in horror from this false trust, for it is precisely that which destroys the only way of salvation: trusting in the person and work of Christ alone.

Paul's Pedigree

"Do-it-yourself-religion" is a surprisingly common style of worship. Have you ever heard a friend say, "Well, I'm just as good as my neighbors"? This attitude has much in common with the religious sytem Paul sharply attacked. Behind it is the plea: "Look at my pedigree. Look at my box score of accomplishments, Lord. You *must* accept me. See what I am offering You!"

Isaiah said it so well, years before Paul confronted the Judaizers: "All our righteousnesses are as filthy rags" (Isaiah 64:6). The cardinal sin is pride; the attitude that one has so much to offer to a holy God. The real tragedy is that our failings are so miserable, there is no way that, by our own efforts, we can approach a holy God. The good news is that God, through Christ, has reached across to us! Our safety lies in our willingness to throw ourselves completely, without reservation, upon His grace. Offering God pitiful scraps of personal achievement, position, or inheritance, is to miss the point entirely! And it is for this reason that Paul lays bare his personal life.

Verses 4-6 are a catalog of Paul's "prizes." It is as if we have stepped into his office and, with a sweeping gesture, he draws attention to the plaques that adorn the wall and the trophies that fill his shelves. This passage is the kind of list the Judaizers would have fussed over, admiring all these claims upon the favor of God. Paul is reluctant to talk about himself. Only in rare places in all of his writings does he pause to give us details about his own personal life. Only when reference to himself proves useful to the gospel does he resort to such intimate recollections. Let's look in on Paul's survey of his past life.

Paul begins his self-evaluation with the preface: "If anyone has reason to boast, I have more than any Judaizer I know." This is not a boastful claim; it is an honest appraisal of fact. Paul states it to disarm any who might accuse him of spite, envy, or other base motives as he launches his crusade against those who twist the gospel.

Circumcised the eighth day. In the first century, there were really three kinds of adherents to the Jewish religion. First, there were those who had been born into Judaism. These were the children taken to the priest on the prescribed day, exactly 8 days after birth, for the rite of circumcision. Second, there were the "God-fearers," proselytes to Judaism from the surrounding pagan culture. These were the people, like Cornelius, who had been inducted into Judaism as adults and went through the rites of baptism and circumcision. Third, there were the outer-fringe gentiles who were "halfway" proselytes. These attended synagogue services, but were neither baptized nor circumcised. In the Jewish world, those born into the faith had a tendency to pride themselves on a superior status. It was a badge of honor that a proselyte could never quite achieve.

Of the stock of Israel. Paul is referring to the covenant God had made with His chosen people. Romans 11:1 points to this special relationship God had to Israel. A theme running through the entire Old Testament is the faithfulness of God to His people, with whom He has made a solemn agreement, an everlasting covenant. The Jews of Paul's day failed to see that faith in Christ was to be a part of that covenant.

Of the tribe of Benjamin. In our nation, we appreciate the regional loyalties that are part of our rich national heritage. Citizens of each of the 50 states display a kind of proper "pride of place." Few, however, would offer up to God the insistence that He accept them because they were born in Texas, Maryland, or Florida. But in the Jewish world, those descended from the little border tribe of Benjamin considered themselves to be just a little superior to all the other tribes of Israel! Jerusalem and the temple lay within its borders. It had remained loyal to the kingdom of David during the terrible civil war. Saul, the first king of Israel, had been from this tiny tribe. So, Paul says, "I, too, could boast, if I chose, of being a Benjamite."

A Hebrew of the Hebrews. Paul was born into a Hebrew-speaking family. There were two important groups of Jews, from a cultural and linguistic standpoint, in Paul's day. The *Hellenists* had adopted Greek customs, along with the common language of the world. Many of them had forgotten the Biblical Hebrew, the language of the Bible. The *Hebraists* continued to diligently study the Bible in its original tongue. They prided themselves on their loyalty to Jewish tradition.

A Pharisee. The heart of the Jewish Scriptures was the *Law*, the five Books of Moses. It was the religious party of Pharisees who boasted of exactitude and strictness regarding the Law. They were the "fundamentalists" of Judaism. No liberal interpretations for them! Paul was of this group.

Persecuting the church. It was a badge of honor in the Pharisaic world of Paul's day to demonstrate zeal by attacking the opposition. The Christian Church posed a threat to traditional Pharisaism, so Paul, in his blind zeal, accepted a commission to persecute the sect known as Christians. Paul was destined for leadership within Judaism. However, while he was on his way to Damascus to hurt the church, Christ arrested him and his life was radically changed (Acts 9:1-21).

Blameless. Considering the 648 points of the Pharisaic code, the "hedge around the Law," it is a remarkable assertion that Paul makes: he was *blameless.* As far as the outward observance of the Law, Paul could boast that he had made no visible errors. It should be remembered, however, that later Paul came to understand the true nature of sin, and he realized that below the level of actual performance there lies a great iceberg, the motives of the heart (Romans 7). In this passage, Paul does not speak of his achievement in any other than the Jewish legalistic frame of reference. In that sense, and that alone, he could boast of his blamelessness.

What a pedigree! How zealous was this earnest young Jewish scholar; the top student in the class of

Gamaliel (Galatians 1:14)! If sincerity and zeal counted for much, Paul would put many of us to shame. Yet Paul acknowledges that these are poor offerings to present to our matchless Saviour. "Nothing in my hands I bring, simply to thy cross I cling" came to be Paul's song. Herein lies rest, forgiveness, grace, and the full meaning of the good news in Jesus Christ! Every other thing that we may hold up to God and of which we may boast offers nothing but empty expectations.

9

Righteousness by Faith

READ PHILIPPIANS 3:7-11

Every business establishment periodically takes inventory of its stock on hand. This is a way of determining what the health of that business is: whence it has come, where it stands presently, and what direction it seems to be taking. It is an important means of evaluation.

In the life of every individual, it is helpful periodically to reflect on one's own personal spiritual "inventory." Each time a believer partakes of the Lord's Supper, he is encouraged to engage in self-examination (1 Corinthians 11:28). Paul invites us to join him in his own introspection. The verses assigned for our present consideration carry us on an inspection tour of Paul's estimate of where he *was*, where he *is*, and where he is *going*. In the process, we are able to see in bold relief the central values that govern Paul's life.

Past Accomplishments Rejected

Some live in the past. Have you ever visited a former athlete? His trophies and other memorabilia surround him. No longer able to throw the ball like he did in his younger days, he basks in the warm, glowing memories of heroic youthful moments. For such people, their meaningful lives end very early and the rest of adulthood becomes a postscript to the grandeur of those fleeting youthful years. There is something sad about such a scene.

Some people grieve over dark places in the past, never allowing the forgiveness of the Lord to wash the past clean. Others grimly hang on to past glories, unwilling to relinquish the memories and the self-satisfaction felt, and unwilling to lay self aside to invite the Lord to be enthroned.

But how different for the person who learns the lessons appropriate to the various stages of life! Without brooding or dwelling excessively on the past, the wise soul assimilates the lessons to be learned, and then eagerly plunges into the adventure of tomorrow, trusting the Lord to chart the course.

Paul faces his past squarely (Philippians 3:7). Cast in the perfect tense, what Paul "counted loss" at the moment of his initial surrender to the Lord is an action in the past, the impact of which continues right into the present. It is a characteristic attitude of his life, not merely a passing event. In other words, Paul is emphasizing the definiteness of his decision.

What is it he "counted loss"? The "things" to which he refers obviously recalls the catalog of achievements he has just listed in the previous verses. His medals, his trophies, his wall plaques—all are swept away with one decisive renunciation. A sudden transformation is pictured here. Paul did not gradually "reform" over a long period of time. No, he made a dramatic and abrupt about-face. All that he at one time would have gloried in has been brushed aside, and is still brushed aside.

For what (or whom) did he lay aside his past achievements? "For Christ." He could not have it both ways. Either it would be Paul offering up trinkets and tinsel, the trappings of his own religious self-effort, or it would be an absolute surrender of everything for the sake of the Lord. Judaistic legalism and self-righteousness had to go.

A little lad was crying. His fist was caught in a jar of jelly beans. He wanted the candy so badly, but a clenched fistful would not pass through the mouth of the jar. Frustration! He had to let go of the jelly beans to free his hand. Just so, Paul had long before let go of the "jelly beans" of his old life, and in so doing had entered into the freedom of Christ.

A Price to Pay

"The gospel is free." True enough. "Jesus paid it all." Right again. Our righteousness has been made possible by the merits of Jesus Christ alone. We cannot pay for our own sins. This is the great truth of grace.

Yet, there is another side of the story. It is expressed vividly by Dietrich Bonhoeffer in his classic, *The Cost of Discipleship* (New York: Macmillan Publishing Co., 1963). "Cheap grace" Bonhoeffer tells us, is the very foolish attitude that a person can mouth a few religious words, undergo a few perfunctory religious rites, and call himself a Christian, with no thought to the changes in lifestyle that being a true disciple will require. Bonhoeffer tells us that such a person is kidding himself. He is not really a Christian at all!

Bonhoeffer calls for "costly grace." By this he means that, in coming to Christ, one invites the Lord to make whatever demands He desires on one's style of living, thinking, ambitions, plans, and friends. Accepting Christ's "free grace" in this fashion turns out to be costly to the believer. A joyful cost! Paul tells us that all the *gains* (all those things he once boasted of) he now counts as one single, decisive, loss. He has quit counting his credentials and diplomas. All of the things he could pride himself in are thrown into a sack, a cord is wrapped around it, and the entire bundle is cast away. This is what Paul reports in verse 8.

Paul employs strong language in this verse to emphasize his point. All that would support his sinful pride he calls *dung*. This word might better be translated "refuse." It is the table scraps meant to be thrown out, the mud that soils the shoes. It is worthless. Yes, even repulsive.

The excellency of the knowledge of Christ Jesus. This is Paul's way of saying that the experience of knowing Christ is not merely on a higher scale of the same *kind* of religious value as Judaism and its legalism. No, he is saying, "The experience of really knowing Christ in in another league."

It is for this reason that Paul can state the high price his faith in Christ has cost him. He has indeed suffered the loss of all things: his former position in Judaism, his friends, his power and influence, and even his freedom. It has been costly. Yet, there is no hint here of wavering, not a glimmer of wistfulness. For Paul, the decision he made to follow Christ, in spite of harrowing experiences and physical suffering, is joyfully reconfirmed!

Found Out!

Paul turns, in the last clause of verse 8, from the past to his estimate of the future. His passion is to "win Christ." The root word is found in verse 7, "gain." His eye is on the goal. The past is behind him. He is like a runner in a marathon; refusing to look behind, totally absorbed in the task of successfully crossing the finish line. The analogy is mixed. Surely Paul already knows Christ. But here the emphasis is on persistent living, patient endurance, until the day he is ushered into the very presence of the Lord. Then Christ shall be known no longer by faith alone, but by immediate contact (1 John 3:2).

In the meantime, Paul wants his present life to be utterly transparent. "And be found in him" might better be translated: "And be found out to be in Him." The language of this passage conjures up a scene from daily life. The carpenter misses the nail and strikes his thumb instead. Paul wants, in these unguarded moments, to behave in such a way that he does not betray Christ. It is in such moments that the inner reality of one's relationship to Christ is exposed for all to see. Paul's cry is that his subconscious life will be so penetrated by the indwelling Christ that his first impulse under stress will be to praise His name!

An Alien Righteousness

Luther coined a term to describe what Paul speaks about in verse 9. By "alien righteousness" Luther meant a righteousness attributed to one from outside himself. It may be illustrated like this. When you present a credit card to a clerk in a store, the clerk is likely to give you the merchandise you have requested, even though no money actually changed hands. The clerk may check your credit card account to verify its validity but still no actual cash is involved. Now, suppose you discover that someone has credited a sum of money, in your name, toward your account. It is something you did not even earn. In fact, you may not even have deserved it. But somebody has generously made a donation to your account anyway! "Alien money" has been credited to your account.

Just so, the righteousness that belongs to God himself has been credited to our spiritual account! It is not, in this sense, native to us. Yet God sees us not in ourselves but through the blood of Christ. We are wrapped in His righteousness! We could never merit such an award. It is given freely through the death and resurrection of the Lord. And it is registered to our account upon reception of the gift *by faith*.

Starting as Saints

This "alien righteousness" is also given other names. *Justification* is Paul's way of describing this "credit card" salvation (Romans 3:21-31). It is also called "positional righteousness." This means that God considers us to have the position of "perfect righteousness," not by *our* actual perfection, but because we are identified with Christ, who is himself perfectly righteous.

To view this matter from another way, the theologian speaks of "initial righteousness." This means that at the instant one gives his heart to the Lord, he is declared to be wrapped in the perfect righteousness of Jesus himself, *at that very instant*. He does not "grow" into sainthood. He starts out as a saint!

Look at the salutations of Paul's letters. Even to those Christians who required sharp rebuke, Paul accords them the title "saints." (See, for example: 1 Corinthians 1:2, as well as other Pauline salutations.) You start out as a saint! However, it is only fair to add quickly that Paul spends much of his letters in exhortations, warnings, and pleas to believers. He is saying, by this: "You who are declared to be saints, act like it. Don't betray Christ by your poor behavior."

Access!

One further note should be observed here. Since we could never be good enough in and of ourselves to gain access to God, the marvelous access we do enjoy is dependent on God seeing us through the robes of Christ. We are invited boldly into His presence. There is no fear. We need not stand under the wrath of a frowning God. We are under the blood of Christ! (Hebrews 4:16).

Knowing Him

Paul pours out the depths of his inner soul to his close friends, the Philippian readers, in verse 10. You can almost hear him cry out, "That I may know him. . . ." What does this expression mean? Didn't Paul already know Christ as his Saviour? To be sure he did! What he is expressing here is a heart hunger to experience the fullness of a relationship with Christ ever more profound than his present state of "knowing Christ."

Some have used the term *an unsatisfied satisfaction* to describe the quest of the soul thirsting after God. The Psalmist articulated this mood: "As the hart panteth after the water brooks, so panteth my soul after thee, O God" (Psalm 42:1). The soul in moral and spiritual union with Christ testifies to that relationship by crying out for a growing fellowship.

The power of His resurrection. The authority and enabling wrought by Christ in His triumph over the

85

tomb, have been given to the believer to triumph over the devil. The battle is not over for us yet, but He has promised victory over the dominion of sin! Romans 6 describes in vivid detail the dynamics of the victory available to the believer. This authority and power Paul has already entered into, but he wants to make his knowledge of Christ in victory over sin a growing experience in his life.

The fellowship of His sufferings. Paul does not claim that *his* sufferings can compare with the atonement of Christ. Rather, this is his way of saying that he enters joyfully into any suffering occasioned by his witness for Christ. Paul considers it a high honor to suffer on behalf of his Lord who has given him so much (2 Corinthians 4:10).

Being made conformable unto His death. Paul wants to enter into the meaning of Christ's death and resurrection for him. He wants to die to self and experience in ever greater measure the flow of the new life in Christ (Philippians 3:21). He is speaking about the ethical dimension of his own life. Just as Christ died and rose again, so Paul wants to walk in newness of life in his daily behavior. In this way, his life will be conformed to the death and life of Christ.

Resurrection: the Goal

Verse 10 pictures Paul as he considers his immediate daily life. Verse 11 carries us a step further. Paul is aware that the believer is in a battle as long as he is in this world. Not until the resurrection will the contest be officially over! That will be the consummation for the Christian. He will never again be subjected to the stresses and testings faced in this world. This is the state of "final righteousness" for the believer. A fixed and permanent character of righteousness will then be really and truly our true possession. Just as the distant shoreline toward which the boatman steers is kept in view, this is a worthy aspiration to keep before the believer. This final goal is the ultimate quest of those who inherit righteousness by faith.

10

Pressing On

READ PHILIPPIANS 3:12-16

Many years ago, Sammy Morris, an African student, came to the United States to enroll in a Christian college. He died before he finished his college career, but he left an indelible impression on the college family. Sammy lived among the students and teachers in such a way that his life drew people to Christ. He considered himself to be but a beginner in the school of Christian discipleship, and eagerly sought the assistance of those he felt to be far more mature than himself. The irony of it was that his friends and associates recognized in Sammy Morris the very essence of Christlikeness. While he seemed to himself to be far from excellence, it was in this very quality of Christian humility that Christ was most clearly visible!

Here then is a paradox. Those who pride themselves in their holiness and spiritual attainments may, by their very boasting, disclose self-deception and spiritual poverty. Those who recognize their daily dependence on the continuing grace of God in their lives may be demonstrating a posture much more pleasing to Christ. Hungering and thirsting after righteousness is an appropriate condition for all believers. It is a need believers never outgrow in this life. Perhaps, after all, those who are most saintly are least aware of it.

Not Perfect Yet

Beginning with Philippians 3:12, Paul outlines what might be called "the dynamics of spiritual growth." He says two seemingly conflicting things. In verse 12, he denies that he has already attained *perfection*. (A form of the word *telos*, meaning "end" or "destiny." It may also be translated as "perfection" or "maturity," depending on the context. This word and its various forms convey the idea of something moving toward an intended goal.) In verse 15, however, he speaks about "those of us who already are *teleios*" (translated "perfect" in the Authorized Version). On the surface these two verses seem to be contradictory, and a careful examination of them will be necessary to unravel the perplexity.

First, let us reemphasize that verse 12 is a disclaimer of Paul's actual present possession of *absolute perfection*. He was prayed for by Ananias to receive the Holy Spirit (Acts 9:17, 18). He claimed to speak in tongues "more than ye all" (1 Corinthians 14:18). And wasn't he baptized in the Spirit? Certainly. But it is abundantly clear, particularly from Paul's letter to the Corinthians, that the baptism in the Spirit is not a badge of holiness. It is a mandate *to* holiness. Paul even chides some of the Corinthians for being "babes" or even "carnal" (1 Corinthians 3:1-3). Their public manifestations of the Spirit did not convince Paul of their great spiritual maturity. (See 1 Corinthians 11-14.)

Paul is not advocating a diminishing of spiritual gifts in the Corinthian church (1 Corinthians 14:1). He is urging them to match their excelling in the *expressive* domain with inner spiritual development.

Two Spheres

It is as if Paul is telling these Christian friends that there are two spheres in which the Holy Spirit is pleased to work in our lives. First, there is the *interior* sphere. Here the Holy Spirit quietly convicts the believer of sin, of righteousness, and of judgment to come (John 16:8-14). It is the intent of the indwelling Holy Spirit to fashion every believer into the image of Christ. Paul speaks of Christ being "formed in you" (Galatians 4:19).

A helpful passage is Galatians 5:16-23. Here Paul pictures the conflict between those forces that would drive one down (what he calls "the flesh"), and the counteracting force of the Holy Spirit, an ally given to every believer. The Holy Spirit "wars" against the flesh. The result of this interior confrontation is a display of fruit. Paul does not sidestep what he is talking about. He illustrates the fruit of the flesh with a list of sins that runs the gamut from attitudes to overt, gross, physical actions. It could hardly be plainer. Then he follows this painful list of bad fruit with a catalog of Christian virtues, which we call collectively "the fruit of the Spirit" (Galatians 5:22, 23). These are evidences that the *interior* life is being cultivated.

The purpose of the baptism in the Holy Spirit is expressly for witnessing (Acts 1:8). The earliest Christians could not be kept quiet. They turned the world upside down! Everywhere they were scattered, they "gossiped the gospel" (Acts 8:4). It was assumed in the Early Church that converts would be filled with the Spirit. This certainly was the case in Corinth. The *expressive* domain in some areas was rather well-developed. Various gifts of the Spirit to aid in public worship and to enhance the impact of witnessing were in evidence. Yet those who exhibited the *gifts*, or manifestations of the Spirit (see especially 1 Corinthians 12:8-10), were not thereby automatically guaranteed "instant maturity." No, some of them needed to grow up in Christ (1 Corinthians 11, 13).

But, you say, "How could God use an imperfect vessel to give spiritual utterances?" This is a troublesome question, especially to new Christians. Young converts expect pastors and other leaders older in the faith to be spiritually mature, not only in the *expressive* (the more visible and demonstrable), but also in the *interior* sphere (the less visible, the unobtrusive). Unhappily, this is not always the case. What a disappointment to novices in the faith to discover disconcerting discrepancies in the lives of those they have admired at a distance!

On one occasion, while I was pastoring a small church, we had a gentleman in the congregation who was gifted with leading in public worship. He sang and prayed earnestly. What a blessing he was to us all in the meetings. One day in response to a missionary appeal, he wrote a check. Unfortunately, he had insufficient funds to cover that check. In a few days we learned, to our sorrow, that he had been writing bad checks all over town. What an embarrassment to visit this parishioner in jail! His was surely an uneven development. He was obviously in the same category as the first-century Corinthians whom Paul scolded so sharply.

One way to consider this matter of the "two spheres" is to look back at the days of the Lord Jesus Christ on earth and His cluster of disciples. Jesus did not gather disciples who were already perfect. Far from it! What a motley crew they were! And Jesus did not wait until they were fully matured before He sent them out, two by two, on witnessing assignments (Matthew 10:1-15). They were given *power*, but it was not always equally matched with *holiness*.

What shall we say? Is not our task to cultivate both spheres of the operation of the Holy Spirit in our lives? Shall we betray the Lord by attempting to exercise gifts without fruit? Would it not be pleasing to the Lord to match our desire for power and expression with a deep work of grace in the interior of our lives? We need *all* that God wants to do in us and through us!

The Pursuit of God

Verse 12 categorically disclaims Paul's arrival at a state of perfection. The last half of that verse focuses on the other part of the story of Paul's spiritual journey. Literally, "I pursue," he says. He has a goal in view. He wants to "apprehend" that for which he "was apprehended." Fundamental to this picture is Paul's awareness that he has been captured or seized by Christ. This refers clearly to that memorable day on the road to Damascus, when Christ confronted Paul. Once an enemy of Christ, Paul has now been transformed into a passionate zealot for his Lord. "To me to live is Christ," he exclaims (Philippians 1:21; Galatians 2:20).

Paul tells us by this expression that he sees the Christian life as *progressive*. Conversion means literally to "turn around." At conversion Paul made an abrupt about-face and started marching to the beat of another drum! His new journey had begun, but it was far from complete. For Paul, the goal, not yet reached, is to grasp, to seize, that for which Christ Jesus has laid hold of him. That goal, defined more sharply in other passages, is that he may become more and more like his Master. This is what the theologian calls the doctrine of "progressive sanctification." Notice, this is entirely compatible with the doctrine of the baptism in the Holy Spirit, the anointing for service.

Single-mindedness

Verse 13 describes *how* Paul perceives himself in the process of pursuing God. The heart of the passage is caught in the word *forgetting*. We tend to think of forgetting as a single, decisive act. This word, however, is continuous and is paralleled, by contrast, with the continuous act of *remembering*. In other words, Paul says: "I am forgetting my Jewish pedigree and my past achievements even in the Christian journey, and when I am tempted to remember them all over again, I put them out of my mind." His eye is on a distant shore. He will not turn around to survey the past, lest he be tempted to glory in the past or become complacent.

Every day is a new day for Paul. He is grateful for what God has done for him in the past, to be sure. But his intent here is to demonstrate that he is expecting God to be present in each new day. "Morning by morning, new mercies I see," is a fitting motto for Paul.

This has enormous implications for Christian believers today. How frequently Christians are prone to depend on large public worship services for their total spiritual nourishment ("quickie" prayers at mealtimes and at bedtime excepted). Here is a call for regular, daily quiet times. There is as much need for daily Bible reading and prayer as for breakfast, lunch, or supper! This is the practical application of the doctrine of daily, or progressive, sanctification. Single-minded attention to the goal ought to permit 15 minutes a day for continuing to forget what lies behind; that which clutters our minds and hinders like a heavy garment on the serious runner.

The Race

Verse 14 may refer either to a Roman chariot race or, more likely, a footrace, which is a common metaphor in Paul's writings. The last of verse 13 should really be linked to this verse. "Reaching forth unto those things which are before" describes the runner straining every muscle, bending his body toward the goal and the long-awaited prize.

The same word is used in this verse as in verse 12. It is translated "I follow after" in verse 12; it is "I press" in verse 14. In each case it is a strong verb connoting intense effort being expended to reach the desired object.

Picture the runner. He isn't looking around at the competing athletes around and behind him. Only one thing is on his mind, the goal. This forward-looking effort is the classic picture of the Christian life. The runner is not running to *get* saved. Not at all. He is running because he *is* saved. He has been converted ("turned around") and is now energized and motivated to reach forward with every effort to please his Lord. He runs with joy! He runs with confident expectation that he will be rewarded with the prize of God's approval! No fear here. No desperation. It is a delightful experience. It is a picture of a life filled with purpose and meaning, direction and motivation!

And, it is a "high calling." Better translated, it would read, an "upward calling." The result is that the person is bettered for undergoing the effort; it is uplifting. Heaven is the goal. Athletic contests in our society are certainly physically and emotionally beneficial, but the value of earthly pursuits is quite limited. Not this race! It's for keeps! It is of lasting and eternal value.

The Wholeness of Life

Verses 15 and 16 conclude this analysis of the dynamics of Christian growth. Paul uses the key word *teleios* ("perfect") to describe the Christian in this verse. This is the other side of the paradox. He has already insisted that he has not arrived; he is not "perfect." But now he says: "As many as be perfect...." What Paul is saying is that the Christian life *begins* with a *declared righteousness*. (Philippians 3:8. See chapter 9.) This declared righteousness, credited to the account of the believer at the instant of the new birth, is none other than the righteousness of Christ himself. It is perfect. It is not our own, derived from our goodness. It is *imputed* or "charged" to our account through the grace of God. *Faith* is our role in this wonderful transaction.

So, here it is. The believer begins with a perfection that is credited to his account, but in *actuality* he is growing into Christ likeness progressively. It is as if Paul is telling his friends in Philippi: *"Become* what you *are* in Christ."

Consider the young prince in the royal palace. He is destined someday to rule his country. Yet, as a child, he is still learning how to read, and how to behave. If his training program is successful, this little boy who now gets into mischief and spills his milk at the table, will someday master the characteristics and skills of royalty. The little prince is in the process of becoming what he already is. Just so, the believer is born into heavenly royalty. Royal characteristics are being formed in him day by day. Someday, what is now manifested imperfectly, what is not yet always lovely and graceful, will change to royal characteristics. This the Holy Spirit does in the life of children of the King.

Verse 15 exhorts believers to have a mind-set that cultivates the conviction of the Holy Spirit. We are to be "thus minded." And if, in our state of development, there are moments when we are lured into patterns of thought that will lead downward, we are given the promise that God himself will reveal this to us. The Holy Spirit will not easily let us go! If we begin to slip or "backslide," He will nudge us in the right direction. Our task is to be alert to His conviction.

Walking Around

A favorite word in the practical application portions of Paul's epistles is the word *walk*. Almost always he uses the Greek word found in verse 16, the word meaning to "walk around." It connotes not a straight course, as if one were walking from one point to another point, but rather the "traffic pattern" of daily routines—going to and from school, going to work, doing the housework, and other mundane tasks of life. It is a word for the habits of daily life. It is the way we live.

Paul's final appeal is that we should learn to walk on the level of our attainment. As we grow in the Lord, more is expected of us. We are growing up in Christ. Maturity is not merely reaching upward, but "walking around" on ever new plateaus of Christian character. Press on, saint!

11

Living Examples

READ PHILIPPIANS 3:17 TO 4:3

Christianity is triangular. Jesus said: "I am the *way*, the *truth*, and the *life*" (John 14:6). *Truth* is correspondence with reality. What we call "theology" is the attempt to describe reality, as it is revealed in Christ and Scripture, the Living Word and the written Word.

But all Christianity is not embraced in the conceptual, no matter how truly it may be stated. Jesus said: "I am the *way*." He meant by this that one cannot stand apart objectively, in detachment, and simply ponder great truths. At some point, you must "take the plunge." Being "born again" is entering into the *experiential* domain. Willingness to commit your life to Christ, to surrender your will to His, is the stepping-stone *into* reality. There is no other way. Those who are content to sit on the shore, reluctant to jump into the waters of Christian experience, are only spectators in the most important drama of life. Unless you *participate*, you are outside the real thing altogether.

There is also a third dimension. Jesus said: "I am the *life*." True ideas are important as a means of distinguishing right notions and values from wrong notions and values. Vital, living experience makes such realities personal and real. However, one may *know* truth and even *experience* reality in Christ,

97

but not always *live* according to truth. Ethical living is not exactly automatic.

To be sure, a genuine child of God will have a new desire, a new motivation; he will want to please his Lord. But "growing up in Christ" does not come immediately or always easily. Old patterns, old habits of living, and old values must be consciously sloughed off. New patterns must be learned and modeled. It is good to know that the Holy Spirit has been given to believers to convince them about aspects of living. He is pleased to take the truth of the Bible, truth centering in the Lord Jesus Christ, and bring it to bear on the believer. We do not struggle alone in our own weakness, our humanity, our frailty. The Paraclete has come to help us to "live Christianly"!

The passage before us is an *ethical* pasage. It has to do with a style of living that is appropriate to the new life in Christ. It is intensely practical. It is cast in the *imperative* mood. It is a serious challenge to take the Christian life and influence into the home, the school, and the factory.

Paul's Example

Paul makes what appears on the surface to be a rather arrogant, egotistical appeal. "Follow me" (Philippians 3:17) sounds a little presumptuous until it is examined more closely. What Paul is really doing is giving concreteness to Christianity. Proper living is not merely adherence to abstract principles or a set of maxims or rules. This is precisely what was wrong with Pharisaism. A serious attempt had been made by the Jews to anticipate every conceivable human circumstance, and then to establish a law for that occasion. Jesus showed how wrong this approach to living is. One can meticulously observe the details of rules, yet miss the heart of the matter in the process.

Paul is making it clear in this passage that there is a real connection between a style of living and the great truths about the Christian experience that he has just expressed in the preceding section. (See chapter 10.) However, Paul wants the reader to be very clear that choices have to be made by the believer; right living is not accidental or automatic. And those choices must be made in the concreteness of daily life. Merely an intention to keep the right rules is not enough; there must be a conscious desire to model one's behavior after good examples.

Of course, the highest and best model is the Lord Jesus Christ himself. This Paul reiterates in Philippians 2:5-11. It is a constant theme in his writings. Jesus is the supreme Example.

Paul also understands that Christians are themselves examples to others. He sought to live out the truth before the Philippians while he was with them. He was a "living epistle." For Paul, his whole life was wrapped up in Christ. He did not say one thing with his lips and another with his actions. He did not claim perfection (see the previous chapter), but insofar as he was following Christ, he invited his readers to examine and to emulate his life. There is no arrogance here, for his constant reminder is that he is a trophy of the grace of God (Ephesians 2:8, 9).

You might be surprised if you knew how many people are watching your life. You have an influence of which you may not be fully aware. Can you picture yourself in Paul's situation? Would you be willing to invite others to inspect your life? Would you want them to live the kind of life you do? Influence is an awesome Christian responsibility—and a glorious opportunity to share the transforming power of Christ with others. Our greatest task is to make room for the Holy Spirit in our lives. It is *His* role to aid in conforming us to the image of Christ!

The Community

We do not live as islands in the sea. An important emphasis in Paul's teaching is the community of believers. This is particularly featured in Romans 12, 1 Corinthians 12 to 14, and Ephesians 4. There are also implications of the importance of the "family of God" laced throughout the entire New Testament. In verse 17, Paul admonishes the believers in Philippi not just to follow him, but to *join others* in following him. It is a group process. Can you picture what Paul envisions? He visualizes a cluster of believers helping, encouraging, and supporting one another in the great enterprise of learning to live Christianly. They are not alone! Not only is the gentle Holy Spirit present, but they also minister to each other.

Notice Good Models

Some people are prone to look for every flaw in those around them. Negative persons are likely to find something to grumble about no matter where they turn. The cup is always half empty for them, while for others it is half full.

Paul, in verse 17, is not advocating blindness at all, but is encouraging a set of mind that is on the lookout for constructive aspects of living in others which we can model. "Mark them," he says. "Notice them closely," we could translate. In the community of faith, there are others who exhibit Christlike characteristics. Their example is a ministry to believers. Paul exhorts his readers to allow themselves to be ministered to by such model Christians!

We would do well to look for positive traits of Christian character among our colleagues. It doesn't hurt either, to acknowledge these good points from time to time. Our response to good influences may in turn be encouragement to those going about the business of living for Christ.

Young converts can be helped by the example of others in additional ways. Have you considered sharing a Christian biography with a new convert? The testimony of intimate personal acquaintances is very important to young converts, but the circle of influences can be immeasurably widened by exposure to the wealth of excellent books available in any good Christian bookstore. Vivid, concrete stories of the power of God to change habits of living are important in helping young converts understand what it means to live Christianly.

Once again, here is Paul's favorite ethical word: *Walk! Peripatein* means literally "to walk around." It captures the idea of "daily living." This is the dimension of Christian life that deals with the ordinary, the commonplace, the nitty-gritty. Paul is telling us, in his own way, that we are to look for good examples among us: those who take Christ into their homes, their places of business or study, and their leisure time. Mark these, not only in the church services, but also out on the streets of daily life. Those who follow Paul as he follows Christ, are the ones to focus our attention upon.

The Walk of Destruction

Verses 18 and 19 are a kind of digression. To make his positive point clear, Paul finds it useful to describe with painfully vivid language the opposite side of the story. His point is that some, who evidently call themselves Christian, "walk"—but in a manner that is a betrayal of Christ. He has in mind professing Christians whose intellectual grasp of spiritual truth is not matched by a vital experience with Christ, and is certainly not expressed in an obedient style of living appropriate to the Cross. Whether these betrayers of Christ are Judaizers or pagan gentiles who have carried their careless and immoral ways of living into the church is not clear. Paul is opposed to both. (See Galatians 3 and 4, and 1 Corinthians 5 to 7.) They are the opposite of what he has described in the previous verse. They are *not* to be followed.

There is a stark realism in the way Paul paints the character and destiny of superficial "Christians," those who follow Christ in name only. Paul has told them in Philippi before about such fraudulent living. In each case, Paul could not talk about such people without tears. He is grieved for their sakes, but also because of what they do to Christ and His cause. Here is a good model for us. Paul's example of looking at "enemies of the cross" through tears is a picture of tenderness, concern, and sorrow. He exhibits no glee. And he is not vindictive. The love of Christ shines through.

To live hypocritically is to face destruction. It is serious business. Who are these people? "God is their belly, [their] glory is in their shame, [they] mind earthly things." Today we would call such people *hedonists*; those who are self-centered and demand immediate gratification of sensual appetites. "Grab all the gusto you can, since you only go around once!" is the blaring television commercial. "Beware of any who would give a Christian veneer to materialistic or sensual styles of living," Paul would tell us today. How many Christians eagerly listen to soothsayers who promise "earthly things" in the name of the Lord.

A Christian World View

Verses 20 and 21 paint a positive Christian perspective, in sharp contrast to the digression of the preceding two verses. The word *conversation* could be translated just as easily "citizenship," "behavior," or "style of living." The stance of the believer is an upward look. His motivation, his source of supply, and his goal are not in this world, but beyond it! He is "heaven-oriented." All earthly values and relationships are seen through that awareness. And at the center of that upward gaze is the longing for the Lord Jesus Christ!

These verses are prophetic. They look to the future. Paul pictures the day when Jesus will come again. The body, now subject to pain and even death, will be transformed. It is a reminder that Christ, who conquered sin and death at Calvary, has not yet seen all things put under His feet. We are still in the trenches, doing battle with a defeated enemy who has not yet quit a hopeless fight.

But Paul calls the reader's attention to the "big picture." Our present concern, with its battles and stresses, is to be viewed in light of future victory. "Keep your eye on the goal," he is telling us. "Keep your eye on the leader!" Authentic Christian living comes from persistently, daily observing our Model. By prayer and reading the Bible, by observing Christ at work in our colleagues, our vision of Christian living will be sharpened.

Paul's Joy and Crown

The last chapter in Philippians begins with a kind of notice that a conclusion is imminent. "Therefore," Paul begins. Based on his exposition of the dynamics of Christian experience, and his appeal to imitate the good examples of Christlike character they see about them, Paul now furnishes some practical-application imperatives. Some are general; others are particular.

The general appeal of 4:1 is an oft-repeated call to "stand fast in the Lord." Couched in warm, endearing terms, this verse captures the heartbeat of the apostle. "My brethren dearly beloved and longed for, my joy and crown, . . . my . . . beloved." What a cascade of tender words! Even though Paul is in the midst of giving numerous exhortations, he makes it clear that he doesn't write out of anger or keen disappointment, but out of appreciation and concern.

The central appeal is to "stand." In effect, he is saying: "You are in a spiritual battle, but you are going to make it. Hold steady. Keep on doing what you are already doing." It is reminiscent of the great passage found in Ephesians 6:10-20, which pictures a scene drawn from the Roman military world.

How delightful that in this buoyant Epistle Paul should inject the concept of joy even into a battle scene. The Philippians are Paul's joy, his crown (reward). The essence of Christianity is to live—and to give to the point of death—for others. Christ first, others second, and self third! Jesus—Others—You—the acronym spells JOY!

Trouble in the Choir

Two women in the church at Philippi were not getting along together. No one names daughters

Euodias or Syntyche today! They are the one cloud over the church at Philippi. They wouldn't talk to one another, or if they did, they were antagonistic to each other. Can you imagine! Ladies throwing song-books in the Philippian choir! Well, at any rate, it is a very human picture of real people. Paul does not gloss over this painful rupture of fellowship. He admonishes them to get over their squabble *in the Lord*. Important to the health of the whole church are the interpersonal relationships of the various members within the family of God.

Helpers in the Gospel

Verse 3 is a somewhat broader appeal for cooperative labor, already begun in the church, to continue. Paul appeals to an unknown individual, called "true yokefellow," or perhaps this was really his name. *Syzygos* is exhorted to assist the women who had taken such an important role in the early days of the Philippian church. Evidently they were needing more support. Paul hastens to include someone by the name of Clement, and other "fellow laborers" who are listed as part of the sacrificial community of faith who are to be commended. They, together, are honored by having their names "in the book of life."

In Old Testament passages, intertestamental literature common to the Jews, and in various places in the New Testament (particularly the Book of Revelation), this phrase is employed. It is a way of expressing God's pleasure in the faithfulness of His children, especially those who have endured suffering for His name. Paul wants it made clear that those who have been patient followers of his example and teaching, and thus of the Lord himself, are thus honored for living Christianly.

12

Prescription for Positive Living

READ PHILIPPIANS 4:4-9

He whistled while he worked. Frank Lindquist was a lad of 14 when my father and his brothers first encountered him. Frank washed milk bottles in the family dairy. While he worked, his newfound faith in Christ burst out in joyful sound. It was infectious!

Frank's influence, although he was just a lad, made a deep impact on various members of my family. His merry whistle was an instrument used of God to draw them to a vital relationship with Jesus Christ. Years later, Frank and my Uncle James became the first Assemblies of God pioneers in the state of Minnesota. Frank, the radiant, whistling bottle washer, went on to become a college president and district superintendent. Early in life he had found a useful prescription for abundant, successful living.

Nearing the conclusion of his letter to the Philippians, what can Paul tell his dear friends that will help them the most? The passage under consideration gives us five significant challenges which form a prescription for positive, successful living.

Rejoice!

"Rejoice in the Lord always: and again I say, Rejoice" (v. 4). A bit strange, you may say, to *com-*

mand joy? Several observations should be made. First, there is in this command a strong appeal to keep the foundation of joy uppermost. It is more than whipping up enthusiasm. It is more than the "bootstrap theology" of some contemporary "positive thinking" hucksters. It reaches far beyond that. It fastens attention to the Lord, the Giver of joy.

But let us examine joy itself. Joy and peace are related concepts. So, too, are faith and trust. Here's a little math to try out. "Faith is to joy as trust is to peace." Both faith and joy are active words. Faith is a strong confidence that liberates the individual for action. Trust is the other side of faith. It is the kind of confidence in the Lord that allows the soul to relax in the midst of storms. Each is a dimension of a strong bond between the individual and his Lord.

Similarly joy is an expression of active confidence in the Lord. It is related to achievement, action, and motion. It is a way of describing the soul set free, exhilarating in its Lord; freed to achieve and to radiate the goodness of God. Just as joy may be pictured as the manifestation of active faith, so peace is the corollary of trust. The soul at rest has the tranquility appropriate to the one who is relaxed in the knowledge that God is in charge!

Command joy? Certainly! Paul is saying: "Let the world know that you have strong confidence in your Lord. No circumstance is too great to dull your expectation. Live so that others will know you really believe that your God makes a difference!"

This might be considered a pious platitude were it not for the fact that Paul had triumphed over great obstacles while he was with his readers in Philippi. Neither they nor he would soon forget that dramatic night when the earthquake shook the city jail (Acts 16:25, 26). Consider, too, the circumstances out of which Paul writes. Imprisoned yet another time, he has learned that God can supply joy in the most discouraging of life's situations. It is out of such dark times that the light of God's grace shines the more brilliantly.

Forgive!

"Let your moderation be known unto all men" could be stated in one word, "Forgive." Paul is exhorting his Philippian friends, who indeed have known persecution and misunderstanding, to display the largeness of spirit that reaches across to those doing wrong, expressing forgiveness and compassion. Again, such a large-hearted attitude is an expression, like joy, of great faith in the Lord. Only those with a great confidence in their Lord have the capacity to really go about forgiving those who have hurt and wounded them. Jesus was like that. Paul was learning to do this, too. It is a powerful witness for the Lord!

Some years ago, in our home church, a wife learned the meaning of this challenge. Her husband was not vicious, but he did nothing to encourage her spiritually and he would have nothing to do with the church or with God. Frequently she invited him to the Lord's house, but always the answer was "no." Patiently she went about her life, being as faithful and loving as she could, never chiding or rebuking her husband. But, as the years wore on, she invited him to church with less regularity. After all, he never chose to go anyway. But she lived patiently and lovingly with him, nonetheless.

One night, after more than 20 years of this, she thought she would ask him one more time to go to church with her. She nearly fainted when he said,

"Yes, I think I will." That night he did go to church. He gave his heart to the Lord, and their home was dramatically transformed. What wore him down? Her gentle, forgiving spirit eventually caused him to see the power and reality of Christ. It is, indeed, another dimension of faith, of positive living for Christ.

"The Lord is at hand" is Paul's reminder that the sufferings of this present world will someday be over, and at the end of the age the Lord will reward the patient and forgiving. It is an obvious reference to the second coming of Christ. Strong confidence in the Lord's return is an encouragement to believers who are traveling through the valley of discouragement and difficulty.

Stop Worrying!

"Why pray when you can worry" is the motto of some Christians. "Be careful for nothing" could be paraphrased, "Stop being anxious about things, anything at all." The appeal is directed to earnest Christians who may be inclined to be sensitive and overly scrupulous. The devil delights to rob earnest Christians of their joy by whispering insinuations in their ears such as, "You have not done enough!" or "What do you think so-and-so will think of what you said?"

Anxiety is the key issue here. Fretting about imagined problems robs the believer. This verse is not meant to relieve the believer of *normal* cautions and the need for normal preparation. It is, however, clearly intended to elevate the sights of the believer to a God who is sympathetic, patient, and compassionate. God is not a "cosmic ogre" just waiting to catch us in some petty fault so He can dash us into ruin! No, He is quite the opposite! He stands ready to hear the cry of His children, to rush aid to those in need, to bind up the hurts of the suffering.

The Protected Mind

To teach the positive way to meet the crises of life, Paul directs the Philippians to the ministry of prayer. He does not evade problems. He does not "wish" them away. No, Paul aids the believer to face the harshest difficulties of life head-on—but not alone. Through the ministry of prayer, the believer has access to the throne of grace, to help from God himself. When in need—stop worrying and start praying!

A whole theology of prayer is packed into verse 6. Let us examine some of the words Paul marshals for his exposition of a life of prayer. The first word for prayer he uses is a word employed to describe prayer in general. It is simply "talking to God." It is always used of conversation between the believer and God. It is a way of life, a two-way street.

Encompassed within the larger picture of prayer as conversation with God, Paul lists three specific forms of praying. *Supplication* conveys the idea of one in need calling out for help. It is an emphasis on the dependence of the believer on His God for every kind of need. It is a fitting and proper relationship. An act of trust is to acknowledge that we are, after all, terribly dependent creatures. It is a basic and proper stance of the believer before God.

Requests is precise. The word is not a vague, generalized sense of dependence; it goes beyond that to articulate specific, clear, definite needs (1 John 5:15). Frequently we may be tempted to think God

110

has either not heard our praying or He is not interested in answering us, but part of the problem may be that we have not been specific with God. The Lord clearly appealed for specificity in prayer (Luke 11:5, 9, 10).

Prayer is not merely begging God for needs to be met. It is a relationship of a child to a loving Father. In a vital prayer life, the cultivation of worship is important. Worship includes praise, which is the acknowledgment of who God really is. Although neither worship nor praise is actually stated in this passage, the word *thanksgiving* conveys much the same thought. To be thankful speaks of communion with God, appreciating Him for himself and His infinite perfection. Acts 13:2 uses the helpful language, "ministered to the Lord."

What is the result of not worrying, and praying properly? Verse 7 takes us to the imaginative figure of an ancient city under siege. Instead of the inhabitants of the "city of prayer" being anguished and distraught by fear of imminent disaster, they are "garrisoned about" with the peace of God that goes beyond human comprehension! The army of the Lord is at hand to protect the "heart" and the "mind" from the savage assaults of the enemy. "No weapon that is formed against thee shall prosper" (Isaiah 54:17) is effectively repeated in this beautiful word picture painted by Paul.

Think!

"You are what you think!" The mind feeds on ideas much as the body feeds on physical nourishment. In our day, some are very concerned about proper diet, and rightly so. Our physical and mental well-being are not only intimately interrelated, but also our whole being is affected by such physical aspects of life as diet and exercise.

What is not always equally considered, however, is that what we "feed" our minds also has a powerful impact on our whole being—body, mind, and spirit. Long before our modern psychology and psychiatry, Paul understood the importance of a healthy mind.

"What are you feeding on?" Paul asks. He supplies a diet for believers. The items in the mental bill of fare deserve at least brief comment.

True. That which corresponds to reality. The believer need not escape reality by flights into fantasy. He can face reality. This does not mean that fantasy, such as that written by C. S. Lewis or J. R. Tolkien is wrong for believers. They use imaginative language as a means of communication. The point Paul makes here is that one need not fear reality. He need not "cop out" with recourse to drugs or alcohol to cope with reality.

Honest. This term really means "honorable" or "dignified," as opposed to the cheap and tawdry. Instead of rummaging in the garbage, enjoying the gossip mongering that threatens many Christian groups, the successful believer will avoid dabbling in the destructive, the vicious, the rumor mills, the wells filled with poison. It is a good practice to be a committee of one to steer conversations above the backbiting and the critical. Those who wallow in this mire defile their own spirits, as well as risk injuring others.

Just. Really, "righteous." The idea clearly is that one is going to be a healthier Christian if he is continually filling his mind with positive values, things that are of the "righteous" order, in contrast to unrighteousness. I am convinced that a Christian cannot grow strong and constantly fill his mind with the bill of fare offered by the contemporary cinema or even the pollution offered American families through the television set. Christians ought to be judicious and selective in their viewing, just as they should guard what they read. One need not wallow in a pigsty to understand how to care for pigs.

Pure. This probably has direct reference to sexual purity. In a pagan society that debased sex and the family, the Christian of Paul's day had to exercise great care to rid himself of values destructive to spiritual life. The Christians in Corinth were not the only ones exposed to corrosive influences. Moral failures do not suddenly occur; they are cultivated first in the mind before they are manifested in actual behavior.

Lovely. The Christian is on his way to becoming more fully what God intended him to be. Christian life lifts and ennobles man. The word here is best understood as "pleasing" or "attractive." In one sense, the Christian is most truly Christian when his sensitivities are elevated, when his manners are more gracious, when he becomes more refined as a human being. The coarse, the cheap, and the raucous are demeaning. Good manners are not a "sissy" characteristic for the Christian. Good manners are the genuine mark of caring for others, of demonstrating awareness of others' needs. The Christian does well to cultivate the nobler virtues.

Good report. Here again is a repetition of the concept of avoiding gossip and rumor.

In summary, Paul says: "Think [deeply] on these things."

Do!

The final appeal is to put the new life in Christ into action. Do! What the readers have seen and experienced, what they have seen modeled in Paul, must be lived out. This is the way to successful living. Mere theorizing will not do, it must be lived out in daily life. Do it!

13

Sufficiency in Christ

READ PHILIPPIANS 4:10-23

A gospel chorus familiar to many repeats this assertion: "He is all I need." Paul's great message to the Philippian Christians reaches its climax in the last verses of chapter 4. It can be summarized briefly by the words of that chorus.

The joy Paul has come to realize in Christ has withstood the battering and bombardment of the deepest difficulties man can experience. Neither prison, nor treacherous colleagues, nor the threat of death itself can sink him! He has learned that strong confidence in the risen Lord can sustain the believer in the midst of the greatest crises of life. Paul can report with assurance, tested in the laboratory of life, that his sufficiency is in Christ *plus nothing*.

How frequently we are prone to sigh, "If only this circumstance were different, *then* I would be content." And that is just the point Paul wants to share with his dearest friends, the Philippian Christians, who, like him, have endured considerable affliction. Those who are going through hard places need to know that Christ is able to sustain them, no matter what they may be called on to endure in this world. The Christian can live triumphantly. Circumstances can be transcended. When others are going to pieces, the Christian's quiet confidence becomes a strong testimony to the reality of the indwelling Christ.

Christ *plus nothing!* This is the gospel in its finest hour. Here is faith at work in the rough and tumble of a broken world. Let us look in on Paul as he takes us into the inner sanctuary of his heart and shares his deepest and most tender feelings and concerns.

Appreciation

Verse 10 calls the reader back to the ostensible occasion for which the Book is written: the arrival of the messenger from Philippi laden with gifts from the church for their beloved apostle Paul. Paul receives their gifts as a blessing arranged by the Lord. His rejoicing goes beyond mere human sentiment. He is, to be sure, grateful to the Philippians for their generosity to him. But his highest tribute to them is to acknowledge that they have been instruments of God to minister to his need. His rejoicing is in Christ. It is Paul's way of reporting that he sees Christ at work in all the variegated circumstances surrounding his life.

Just as Christ was able to work out His purposes in Paul's mission to the gentile world through the apparent defeat of imprisonment (chapter 1), so, in a far different way, Christ is working through Paul's friends to nourish and sustain him. The Lord is not limited by circumstances—He can turn darkness into light. Here, however, Paul sees the kindness of the Philippians as a direct pipeline from heaven to him.

In this passage Paul reminds the Philippians that their care and concern for him have finally reached him. Evidently, according to the last clause in verse 10, the Philippians found it difficult to catch up with

Paul. They had been hindered in previous attempts to minister to his need. One is tempted to think that the fault was not theirs, but perhaps Paul's. His missionary "newsletters" may have been sporadic and tardy. The tone of the verse certainly does not blame the Philippians for their negligence of him. At any rate, their persistent concern for him has borne fruit. And Paul is grateful, not only to them, but also to the Lord who prompted them to aid him in his time of need.

Contentment

Ours is a restless age. Stress brought on by frenzied activity sells billions of tranquilizers. Anxiety is a mark of the age. To those caught up in the hectic pressures of modern society, Paul's message in verse 11 is like a beacon in the stormy night.

Paul tells the readers that he has not been crushed with pressing anxiety, as they had feared. To be sure, he was "in want." We do not know precisely what his needs may have been. It is possible that financing the Roman court case was a heavy drain on his resources. He had a material need of sufficient magnitude that the Philippians were distressed by it.

But Paul had learned one of the great lessons of life—*contentment*. The word Paul uses in this verse is unique in the New Testament. It is found elsewhere in the literature of Paul's day to describe the quiet serenity of a "self-made" man, one who exhibits the Stoic ideal of stability in the midst of chaos. Here Paul goes far beyond the Stoic idea of learning by human endeavor the discipline of will that produces firmness of character. The passage at hand is cast in the aorist tense, indicating a decisive event. When Paul found the Lord, he was given a new character, a new power, and a new peace. *His* contentment, then, rested in the indwelling Christ, not in his self-development. For Paul, a flood of peace rushed upon him in an instant; the results of which endured throughout his life. Paul has just testified to "the peace of God, which passeth all understanding" (Philippians 4:7), an experience he wishes to share with his readers.

To Have or Have Not

Some people find it very difficult, once they have enjoyed comfort and position, to endure privation if circumstances later require it. Some suffer from a "martyr complex" as well. These dear souls go about with a forlorn air, looking on the dark side of all things and expecting the worst. They expect that God can only be found in the grim and difficult. The will of God for them is always the dismal way. Enjoyment is impossible, since God is "down" on anything delightful. Then there are those naive souls who wear a perpetual grin, assuring one and all that in the will of God there can be no pain, no suffering, and no hindrance. To admit to reverses for them is admission of "lack of faith." God's way is instant and continuous prosperity.

What is common in each of the above perspectives on life is the delusion that circumstances are central to one's well being. Paul is not resentful of lost affluence and position. He is not expecting the worst all the time, either. Nor is he denying the reality of present poverty and difficulty. He is delivered from these attitudes. He can be abased or he can abound. He can walk or he can ride. It doesn't matter. He has learned to receive gratefully what God provides for him, resting in the assurance that God is in charge of his affairs. Few lessons in life are as helpful as this.

Strength in Christ

Paul, having stated his position regarding the changing and undependable circumstances of life, qualifies his message of contentment expressed in verse 12 with an additional comment in the following verse: "I can do all things through Christ which strengtheneth me." Three things need to be noted here.

First, Paul makes it clear that his contentment is not to be equated with total passivity. He is not using his repose in Christ to excuse himself from meaningful exertion and strenuous activity. He is not intending that the Philippians think he is advocating a listless approach to life. This is not a substitute for earnest planning and judicious stewardship of time and opportunity. The emphasis in verse 13 is on Paul's *doing*. He rests securely in the knowledge that what God has called him to achieve, He will not allow to be frustrated by circumstances. Paul's peace and contentment are in the assurance that Christ is greater than any human or demonic roadblock. Paul has his eye on fulfilling the will of God successfully. Here is confident action!

Second, Paul's testimony is anchored in the knowledge of God's will. Paul is not saying, "Anything that pops into my head, I can do." That is fanaticism. Paul is not advocating foolish venturing against the face of all wise counsel and good judgment. No, he has in mind the believer who has a strong conviction about the will of God, about the course of action to be taken. Paul reports that the believer need not fear that God will let him down. He will see the believer through, in spite of reverses and apparent failures. When God calls a Christian to a task, His calling carries with it the enabling for its completion. It is important, then, to make time for communion with the Lord to hear from Him what *His* will is. Then, and only then, can one claim the testimony of Paul in Philippians 4:13.

And, third, it is important to bear in mind that the sufficiency Paul rejoices in relates directly to his place in Christ. It is not "self-sufficiency." Paul is not a superman. His key to successful achievement of God's purposes for him lies squarely in his sense of total dependence on the Lord.

Sharing

In verses 14 through 16, Paul returns to the matter of the generosity of the Philippians. He expresses his appreciation for them by using a word translated in the Authorized Version as "communicate." It is a compound word containing the root idea, *koinonia*, "fellowship." So, they are pictured as "sharing in fellowship" in regard to Paul's sufferings. In so doing, they "have done well" (Philippians 4:14).

Paul has just disclosed in the immediately preceding verses his knowledge in Christ on how to ride out the storms of privation and stress. Here he hastens to add that, in spite of his serenity in the Lord, they have done a good thing in rushing to his aid. These concepts are not contradictory. *Both* are valid. God has given Paul peace; God has used the Philippians to minister to his need.

Verses 15 and 16 allude to the time when Paul

arrived in Philippi for the first time to preach the gospel (Acts 16). This was "the beginning of the gospel." Paul reminds them that, at the time of his departure from that region, no church had the precious bond of reciprocal "giving and receiving" that existed between the Philippian church and Paul. He gave to them spiritual ministry, which they were eager to receive. In return, they gave material sustenance to Paul to assist him on his journey, for which he was grateful. This concept of material support for spiritual ministry is articulated by Paul in such passages as Galatians 6:6 and 1 Corinthians 9:3-12. It is a two-way street.

And, the giving of the Philippians is commended in yet another way in verse 16. "Once and again" they sent gifts to Paul when he was beyond their city's border. The reference to Thessalonica likely refers to Paul's visit to that city shortly after his departure from Philippi (Acts 17). More than once they located Paul to assist him in his need. It was a virtual habit of life. Paul assures them that their latest gift sent to him through Epaphroditus is but an extension of this warm-hearted generosity.

A Good Bank Account

Verses 17 and 18 contain at least four separate bookkeeping terms. Paul is avoiding the appearance of greed. Although he sincerely appreciates the goodness of heart of his readers, he wants to make it clear that he is not thanking them in hope of further gains from them. Rather, he is willing to receive their generosity, since this will be credited to their account. The term *fruit* might just as well be translated "interest." Then it would read something like: "I am desiring interest which will make your account grow."

Verse 18 continues with the same business-world imagery. Paul uses a word commonly employed for a receipt. "I have a receipt showing that I have received all I need" conveys the idea of this verse.

The gift the Philippians sent to Paul is described by him in an imaginative way, using Old Testament language drawn from the temple sacrifices. "An odor of a sweet smell, a sacrifice acceptable, well-pleasing to God" exalts the transaction to the level of spiritual ministry. Their gift is *more* than "good business." It is appreciated as an act of devotion to the Lord himself.

The Supply of All Need

Philippians 4:19 is one of the most oft-quoted passages in the whole of Scripture. It is a sweeping, powerful statement about the provisions of God for His people. "My God shall supply all your need" is, of course, directed specifically to the Philippian church. They have, evidently, given to the point of their own privation and are now in need because of their generosity to Paul. The court costs and the other expenses Paul incurred in Rome were likely substantial. But, because these dear friends had ministered to Paul in the name of the Lord, Paul is able to promise them God's ready supply.

And, what a supply! In harmony with the glorious riches of Christ. A lavish supply! Both material and spiritual needs will be met abundantly, gloriously! Not somehow, but triumphantly.

Although this promise is directed especially to the Philippians, we too can enter into this provision. Those who are submitted to the lordship of Christ, who give of themselves in loving fashion to the needs He presses upon them, may certainly be assured that it is impossible to outgive God! Our God is gracious and generous. It is His very nature!

Benediction

Now we come to the end of this delightful Book of joy. Verses 20 to 23 contain final words of farewell. The Christians in Rome join with Paul in these warm greetings to the most beloved congregation in the New Testament world.